# Really Interesting Stuff You Don't Need to Know

# Volume 2

*1,200 Fascinating Facts*

David Fickes

# Introduction

By nature, I tend to collect trivia without trying. Until relatively recently, I had never sought out trivia; however, after creating a holiday trivia presentation for a community party and then showing it at one of our fitness studio's spinning classes, I found myself creating weekly trivia. The cycling clients enjoyed the diversion of answering questions while they exercised, so I continued.

I have tried to ensure that the information is as accurate as possible and verified against multiple sources, and to retain its accuracy, I try to avoid facts that can change quickly with time. This book is intended for people who prefer to read interesting facts rather than quiz themselves. Since the information isn't in a question and answer format, it also allows different types of facts that aren't as well suited for a quiz format.

There are 1,200 fascinating facts covering a wide range of topics. I have also incorporated the who, what, when, where, and why behind the facts as appropriate. This is book 2 of my *Really Interesting Stuff* series; I hope you enjoy it, and if you do, look for other books in the series.

# Contents

# Facts 1-300

1) On April 23, 2005, the first video ever uploaded to YouTube was *Meet Me at the Zoo.* It was 19 seconds of a boy explaining that elephants have long tusks.

2) Blind people still dream. People who were born blind or lost their sight at four to five years old or younger don't have visual imagery in their dreams, but people who lost their sight later in life continue to dream with visual imagery as if they could still see.

3) Instead of the five tastes (sweet, savory, sour, bitter, and salty) that humans can detect, whales and dolphins can only taste salty; everything they eat tastes like varying degrees of salty.

4) The Chinese giant salamander is the largest amphibian in the world and can grow to lengths of almost six feet.

5) In traditional vampire folklore, one of their weaknesses is arithmomania, a compulsion to count things. This weakness can be used to defend against them by placing grains of rice or sand out which they will be compelled to count. Therefore, *Sesame Street's* Count von Count's love of counting is part of being a vampire.

6) Hippos don't really swim; they walk underwater. If they are submerged, they don't swim back to the surface; they just walk on the bottom until they reach shallower water. They can hold their breath for five minutes or longer.

7) Goats can develop accents. Researchers found that a goat's accent changed as they aged and moved in different groups; this disproves the idea that their voices were entirely genetic and suggests that most mammals can develop an accent from their surroundings.

8) The superstition of walking under a ladder dates back 5,000 years to the ancient Egyptians. A ladder leaning against a wall forms a triangle

which represented the trinity of the gods to the Egyptians, and it was a desecration to pass through a triangle.

9) Despite having by far the longest coastline of any country in the world, the Royal Canadian Navy only has about 36 ships.

10) In 2014, McDonald's tested bubblegum flavored broccoli to encourage children to eat healthier. The flavor proved confusing to children and was never introduced.

11) The Declaration of Independence wasn't signed on July 4, 1776. It was signed on August 2, 1776; it was adopted by Congress on July 4, 1776.

12) If you complete courses in archery, pistol shooting, sailing, and fencing at the Massachusetts Institute of Technology, you can be recognized as a certified pirate.

13) According to research by Johns Hopkins, medical errors rank as the third leading cause of death in the United States behind heart disease and cancer.

14) Your fingernails grow 2-3 times faster than your toenails, and the fingernails on your dominant hand tend to grow faster than on your other hand.

15) The world's first true ATM debuted at a Barclay's Bank branch in London on June 27, 1967; ATMs wouldn't become common until at least 1990.

16) Three U.S. presidents got married while in office. John Tyler and Woodrow Wilson remarried after losing their wives; Grover Cleveland got married for the first time in the White House.

17) Abel Tasman discovered Tasmania, New Zealand and Fiji on his first voyage, but he completely missed Australia.

18) The burnt part of a candlewick is called the snaste.

19) Almost 1% of the world's population eats at McDonald's each day.

20) Jellyfish are the oldest multi-organ animals in the world. They evolved 550 million years ago and have no brain or nervous system, and their body is 90% water.

21) The loop on a belt that keeps the end in place after it has passed through the buckle is called the keeper.

22) Only about 2% of the islands in the Caribbean are inhabited.

23) Cicadas are the world's loudest insects reaching about 120 decibels which is equivalent to sitting in the front row of a loud rock concert.

24) The singular forms of spaghetti, confetti, and graffiti are spaghetto, confetto, and graffito.

25) Chinese prostitute Ching Shih (1775-1844) is widely regarded as the greatest pirate ever. At the height of her power, she controlled more than 1,500 ships and had 80,000 sailors which was one of the largest naval forces in world history. She robbed and taxed towns and plundered ships along the coast of the South China Sea.

26) A group of pandas is called an embarrassment.

27) Through nuclear fusion, the Sun loses about 4.3 million tons of mass per second as it is transformed into energy.

28) In 1995, astronomers found a gas cloud 10,000 light-years away in the constellation Aquila that contains enough alcohol to make 400 septillion pints of beer.

29) We won't always have the same North Star. In 13,000 years, Polaris, the current North Star, will be replaced by Vega, and 26,000 years from now, Polaris will be back as the North Star. This is because of a change in the direction the Earth's axis points due to a motion called precession. If you think of a spinning top given a slight nudge, the top traces out a cone pattern; that is how the Earth moves on its axis. The Earth bulges out at the equator, and the gravitational attraction of the Moon and Sun on the bulge cause the precession which repeats in a 26,000-year cycle.

30) About 90% of the coal we burn today came about because wood-eating bacteria didn't evolve until about 60 million years after trees existed. For tens of millions of years, all the dead tree material remained intact; trees would fall on top of each other, and the weight of the wood would compress the trees into peat and then into coal. Had wood-eating bacteria been around, they would have broken the carbon bonds and released carbon and oxygen into the air; instead, the carbon remained in the wood. Adding to the coal formation, early trees were tall, up to 160 feet, with thin trunks, fernlike leaves on top, and very shallow roots, so they fell over very easily. This era from 359 to 299 million years ago is known as the Carboniferous Period because of the large amounts of coal formed.

31) Andorra has no standing army but requires by law that the eldest able-bodied man in each household must have a rifle to be used for national protection if needed.

32) Scientists believe that human fingers and toes prune in water due to an evolutionary adaptation where the wrinkles in the skin improve your grip on wet or submerged objects by channeling away water like rain treads on car tires.

33) Despite deaths and injuries, staged train collisions were a spectator attraction from 1896 up until the Great Depression. In 1896, Crush, Texas was a temporary site established for a one-day publicity stunt of a staged train wreck. It was organized by William George Crush, general passenger agent of the Missouri-Kansas-Texas Railroad. No admission was charged, but the railway charged $2 for every round-trip to get to the site; a restaurant served people, and there was a midway, and medicine shows. An estimated 40,000 people attended. For the main event, two unmanned six-car trains crashed into each other at 50 mph. Despite what mechanics had assured, the steam boilers on both trains exploded creating flying debris that killed two people and injured many others. The spectators had been required to observe the collision from a hill 200 yards away, but they still weren't safe from the flying wood and metal. The staged collisions became

popular, and Scott Joplin even wrote the "Great Crush Collision March."

34) Fuggerei in Augsburg, Germany is the world's oldest social housing complex still in use, and the rent for a housing unit has remained the same for 500 years at about $1 per year. It was founded by Jakob Fugger the Younger in 1516 as a place for the needy. The conditions to live there are the same as they were 500 years ago; someone must have lived at least two years in Augsburg, be Catholic, and have become indigent without debt. The rent has always been one Rheinischer Gulden per year as well as three daily prayers for the current owners of the Fuggerei. The housing units are 500-700 square feet with their own street entrance, and the gates to the community are locked every night at 10 pm as they have been since the start.

35) Recent research suggests that ice is slippery because there are loose water molecules on the surface that essentially act like marbles on a floor. Prior theories that it was due to pressure creating a thin layer of water on the surface have been disproven since the pressure would have to be far too great.

36) Sandwiches didn't appear in American cookbooks until 1815.

37) A female octopus can lay tens of thousands of eggs at one time, and when they hatch, she dies. She reproduces only once, and after she lays her eggs, she doesn't eat and puts all her energy into caring for them.

38) Mr. and Mrs. are abbreviations for master and mistress.

39) On January 25, 1979, Robert Williams was the first human killed by a robot. He died when he was hit in the head by a mechanical arm at a Ford casting plant.

40) Camels store water in their bloodstream not in their hump. They can drink up to 20 gallons at a time; the hump is almost all fat and serves as an alternative energy source and helps regulate body temperature. By concentrating fat in the hump as opposed to being spread over their body, they are better able to handle hot climates.

5

41) Due to lava flows from the Kilauea volcano, the Big Island of Hawaii is getting 42 acres larger each year.

42) The three-line symbol you typically find in the upper corner of a screen that you click or tap to get to a menu is called the hamburger button because it looks like a hamburger.

43) Saudi Arabia imports camels and sand from Australia. Camels are a large part of the Muslim diet and are in short supply in Saudi Arabia, so they import camels from Australia which has the world's largest wild camel population. Saudi Arabia also imports Australia's garnet sand because its unique properties make it ideal for sandblasting.

44) Mozart wrote a six-piece canon titled *Leck mich im Arsch* which translates as *Kiss My Ass*.

45) Pittsburgh is the only city where all the major sports team have the same colors; the Pirates, Penguins, and Steelers all use black and gold colors.

46) If you fly directly south from Detroit, Michigan, you will hit Canada. You will fly over Windsor, Ontario before re-entering the United States.

47) Up through the Victorian era, it was common for both boys and girls to wear dresses until the age of seven. The reasons for boys wearing dresses were primarily practical in terms of ease of dressing, potty training, and dresses weren't as easily outgrown.

48) Tootsie Rolls were part of the rations for soldiers in WWII; they were durable in all weather conditions and were good for quick energy.

49) In 1958, Mao Zedong, founding father of the People's Republic of China, initiated a campaign to eliminate sparrows which led to the deaths of 45 million people. He considered sparrows a pest, and through the Great Sparrow Campaign, he ordered all sparrows to be killed. In 1961, up to 45 million people starved to death because the elimination of sparrows led to an explosion in the insect population which ate all the crops.

50) President Rutherford B. Hayes was the first American to own a Siamese cat; the cat was a gift to the president by the American consul in Bangkok.

51) The fax machine is older than the telephone and was patented the same year the first wagon train crossed the Oregon Trail. The original patent for the Electric Printing Telegraph or fax was in 1843 by Scottish inventor Alexander Bain, and the first commercial use of a fax machine was in France in 1865, 11 years before the telephone was invented and the year the American Civil War ended.

52) Up until a 1747 proclamation by Spain's King Ferdinand VI, many Europeans believed California was an island. The misconception started in 1510 when Spanish novelist Garci Rodríguez de Montalvo wrote *Las Sergas de Esplandián* about a mythical island called California. His work formed the basis for naming California, and the name propagated the idea it was an island.

53) Over the entire *Bonanza* television series, the Cartwrights proposed marriage 22 times - Little Joe (11), Hoss (6), Ben (3), Adam (2). A lot of the engagements ended in death.

54) President James Garfield could simultaneously write in Greek with one hand and Latin with the other. He was ambidextrous and taught both languages while attending college.

55) A Swedish mathematician calculated that there are 177,147 different ways to tie the knot of a necktie. The number accounts for variations on exposed knots, wrappings, and windings.

56) Flyting was a poetic exchange of insults practiced between the 5th and 16th centuries. The exchange of insults could get quite rude including accusations of cowardice or sexual perversion.

57) If you smoothed out all the wrinkles in your brain, it would lie flat about the size of a pillowcase.

58) In 1930, Louis Armstrong was one of the very first celebrities arrested for drug possession. He described marijuana as "a thousand

times better than whiskey," and in 1930, he and his drummer were arrested after police caught them smoking marijuana outside the Cotton Club in California. He served nine days in jail but continued using marijuana regularly for the rest of his life.

59) Since the origin of humans, the Sun has only finished 1/1250th of an orbit around the center of the Milky Way Galaxy.

60) There are more insects in one square mile of empty field than there are people in the world.

61) In medieval manuscripts, it is common to see pictures of knights fighting snails; no one knows why.

62) Annually, more than 1.5 million euros are thrown into Rome's Trevi Fountain; the money is used to subsidize a supermarket for the needy.

63) Morton's toe is when your second toe is longer than your big toe; it occurs in 10-20% of the population.

64) French filmmaker Albert Lamorisse (1922-1970) is best known for creating award winning short films such as *The Red Balloon* (1956) which won the grand prize at Cannes and an Oscar, but he also invented the strategic board game Risk in 1957.

65) Volvo invented the revolutionary three-point seat belt used today; they gave away the 1962 patent for free to save lives.

66) On a per capita basis, Alaska produces more serial killers than any other state.

67) There are at least 24 dialects of English spoken in the United States.

68) Worker ants, the most common and smallest ants in any colony who do most of the work, are all sterile females.

69) Due to segregation considerations, the Pentagon's designers included 284 bathrooms, twice the number needed for the anticipated staffing. However, President Franklin Roosevelt issued an executive order banning segregation in federal buildings before the building was

open, so it opened as a desegregated facility and was for a time the only desegregated building in Virginia since state laws required segregation.

70) Rascette lines are the creases on your inner wrist.

71) The first 3D movie was shown in 1922. The film *The Power of Love* premiered at the Ambassador Hotel Theater in Los Angeles on September 27, 1922. It could be shown with a single projector, but it required special glasses for viewing.

72) In Victorian times, photography subjects were encouraged to say prunes instead of cheese. Among other reasons, Victorians thought it was classless to show a big toothy smile.

73) Gold is so malleable that you could create a wire one micron thick that would stretch around the world with just 20 ounces of gold. One ounce, about the size of a quarter, can be beaten into a continuous sheet of about 100 square feet.

74) The ketchup used by McDonald's annually would fill 50 Olympic size swimming pools.

75) In 1916, the first woman was elected to the U.S. Congress four years before women were given the right to vote.

76) Written out in English, eight billion is the second number alphabetically no matter how high you go.

77) Wilmer McLean's homes were involved in both the beginning and end of the American Civil War. On July 21, 1861, the First Battle of Bull Run took place on his farm near Manassas, Virginia. Afterwards, he moved to Appomattox, Virginia to escape the war, but in 1865, General Robert E. Lee surrendered to Ulysses S. Grant in McLean's house in Appomattox.

78) The first recorded strike in history took place in ancient Egypt on November 14, 1152 BC when the artisans of the Royal Necropolis at Deir el-Medina organized an uprising. It took place under the rule of

Pharaoh Ramses III and was recorded on a papyrus that dates from that time.

79) There are 18 countries in the world that don't have any natural rivers - Bahamas, Bahrain, Comoros, Kiribati, Kuwait, Maldives, Malta, Marshall Islands, Monaco, Nauru, Oman, Qatar, Saudi Arabia, Tonga, Tuvalu, United Arab Emirates, Vatican City, Yemen.

80) Alaska has all five of the largest land area cities in the U.S. – Yakutat, Sitka, Juneau, Wrangell, and Anchorage.

81) Mary Shelley came up with the idea for *Frankenstein* in the summer of 1816 while she was staying on Lake Geneva with her future husband Percy Bysshe Shelley and writers Lord Byron and John Polidori. Byron challenged them all to write a ghost story, and *Frankenstein* was published two years later when Shelley was 20 years old.

82) In 1866 in the last battle Liechtenstein ever participated in, they sent out an army of 80 men for the Austro-Prussian War; they came back with 81 men. They had no casualties and picked up an extra soldier along the way.

83) Bombardier beetles have a unique defense mechanism where they emit a hot noxious chemical spray which is produced from a reaction between hydroquinone and hydrogen peroxide which are stored in two reservoirs in the beetle's abdomen. When the solutions are mixed with catalysts, the heat from the reaction brings the mixture to near the boiling point of water and produces gas that drives the ejection. The spray can be fatal to attacking insects. There are over 500 species of bombardier beetles, and they live on all continents except Antarctica.

84) Mount Rushmore got its name from New York attorney Charles Edward Rushmore who visited the Black Hills area in 1884 on business. He asked a guide what the name of the mountain was, and the guide said they would name it now. The name somehow stuck.

85) Pen caps have a hole in them to minimize the risk of children inhaling them and choking to death. It is an international safety standard.

86) The Pacific Ocean is so large that at some points it is antipodal to itself. Two points are antipodal if they are on diametrically opposite sides of the Earth, so at some points in the Pacific Ocean, you could go straight through the center of the Earth and come out the other side and still be in the Pacific Ocean.

87) Historians estimate that Genghis Kahn may have been responsible for as many as 40 million deaths. The population of China fell by tens of millions during his lifetime, and he may have reduced the entire world population by up to 11%.

88) The Slinky was invented by accident by mechanical engineer Richard James in 1943. He was devising springs that could keep sensitive ship equipment steady at sea, and after accidentally knocking some samples off a shelf, he watched as the spring righted itself.

89) The croissant originated in Austria and not France. It started in Vienna, Austria as early as the 13th century as a denser crescent shaped pastry called a kipferl and didn't show up in France in its current form until the early 1800s.

90) Dogs aren't colorblind, but they only have 20% of the cone photoreceptor cells that control color perception that humans have. Dogs see in shades of yellow and blue and lack the ability to see the range of colors from green to red, so dogs see the colors of the world as basically yellow, blue, and gray.

91) During the Victorian period on both sides of the Atlantic, fern mania known as pteridomania was a huge fad. Almost every house had a potted fern; people would collect rare ferns; there were fern books and fern societies, and florists bulked out floral arrangements with ferns.

92) The first motel in the world was opened in 1925 in San Luis Obispo, California; the original room charge was $1.25 per night.

93) Measured by its share of the world's population, the largest empire in history was the Persian Empire which accounted for approximately 44% of the world's population in 480 BC. In contrast, the British Empire accounted for about 23% of the world's population at its peak.

94) Sam Snead was the first PGA golfer to shoot their age in a tournament round; he shot a 67 at the 1979 Quad Cities Open.

95) The Earth weighs about 13,170,000,000,000,000,000,000,000 pounds.

96) Clouds appear to be darker because they are thicker which prevents more light from passing through; thinner clouds allow more light through and appear white. The top of the cloud will still appear white seen from an airplane since the top receives more light. As water droplets and ice crystals in a cloud thicken when it is about to rain, they scatter much less light, and the cloud appears almost black.

97) People have surfed for 8 miles and over 30 minutes continuously riding a wave upstream on the Amazon River. The Pororoca is a tidal bore wave up to 13 feet high that travels up to 500 miles inland upstream on the Amazon River and has become popular with surfers. The wave occurs during new and full moons when the ocean tide is the highest and water flows in from the Atlantic. The phenomenon is most pronounced during the spring equinox in March when the Moon and Sun are in direct alignment with the Earth, and their gravitational pull is combined. The wave can be quite destructive as it moves upriver, and the water is filled with debris.

98) A penny dropped from the 1,250-foot Empire State Building wouldn't kill a bystander below. Due to air resistance, the penny would reach its maximum speed after falling only about 50 feet. When it reached the ground, it would only be moving 25 mph, enough to hurt but nowhere near enough to kill.

99) Frozen seawater contains only about one tenth of the salt content found in liquid seawater because most of the salt separates from the water as it freezes. Seawater freezes at about 28.4 degrees Fahrenheit due to the salt content.

100) In 18th century England, pineapples were so rare and such a status symbol that a single pineapple could sell for the equivalent of $8,000 today, and you could rent a pineapple for the evening to show off to guests.

101) On the animated television show *The Simpsons*, only God and Jesus have five fingers; all other characters have four.

102) New Hampshire consumes more alcohol per capita than any other state; its consumption is 103% higher than the national average and more than one gallon per capita higher than the second highest state, Delaware.

103) When multiple story apartments were first built, the rich lived on the ground floor and not the upper floors. When the Romans first built 9-10 story apartment buildings, wealthier people lived on ground floors since higher floors wouldn't typically have running water or bathrooms and required climbing up multiple flights of stairs. It wasn't until the elevator came about in the latter 1800s that upper floors became status symbols.

104) By area, Vatican City is the smallest country in the world; it is so small that there are 5.88 popes per square mile with just the current pope.

105) If you have a buccula, you have a double chin.

106) Forks were first introduced in Italy in the 11th century; however, they were originally seen as an offense to God since they were considered artificial hands and therefore sacrilegious.

107) The word oxymoron is itself an oxymoron. It derives from the Greek "oxys" meaning sharp or pointed and "moros" meaning stupid,

so the word itself is composed of a contradiction in terms, and it also means a contradiction in terms.

108) The English language is not native to Britain; it is a Germanic language and was brought to Britain in the mid-5th to 7th centuries by Anglo-Saxon settlers.

109) In 1971 after a drilling rig collapsed into a crater in Darvaza, Turkmenistan, engineers set the gases on fire to prevent the spread of methane; they thought it would burn for a few weeks, but it has been burning ever since. The crater is about 230 feet in diameter and 100 feet deep and has become one of the most popular tourist attractions in the country.

110) A strawberry isn't a berry, but a banana is. Botanically, a berry must have three layers: a protective outer layer, a fleshy middle, and an inner part which holds the seeds. It must also have two or more seeds and come from a flower with only one ovary. Strawberries come from a single flower with more than one ovary, making them an aggregate fruit. True berries come from one flower with one ovary and typically have several seeds.

111) Reaching only about two feet in length, the cookie cutter shark's name comes from its unusual feeding method where it gouges out round plugs, as if cut with a cookie cutter, of flesh from larger animals.

112) The smallest thing ever photographed is the shadow of a single atom. In 2012, scientists were able to take picture of the shadow produced by a single atom. Using an electrical field, they suspended the atom in a vacuum chamber and shot a laser beam at it to produce the shadow.

113) No one is born a citizen of Vatican City. To become a citizen, you must work for the city-state. If you lose your job, your citizenship is revoked, and you automatically become an Italian citizen if you aren't already a citizen of another country.

114) Modern humans appeared about 200,000 years ago, but recorded history only dates back about 5,000 years, so about 97.5% of human history is unrecorded.

115) Only about 8% of the world's currency exists as physical cash; the rest is in electronic accounts around the world.

116) Humans have managed to explore only about 5% of the ocean floor.

117) Cats have 32 muscles in each ear and can move each ear independently. They can also swivel and rotate their ears 180 degrees to locate sounds. Humans have 6 muscles in each ear.

118) Boston and Austin are the only two U.S. state capitals with rhyming names.

119) At up to 19 feet long, the king cobra is the largest venomous snake.

120) In his writings, William Shakespeare created over 1,700 of our common words and phrases, more than anyone else by far. He did it by changing nouns into verbs, changing verbs into adjectives, connecting words never used together, adding prefixes and suffixes, and creating original words. Some examples of his creations include: fancy-free, lie low, foregone conclusion, a sorry sight, for goodness sake, good riddance, mum's the word, what's done is done, scuffle, uncomfortable, manager, dishearten, eventful, new-fangled, hot-blooded, rant, with bated breath, laughable, negotiate, jaded, a wild goose chase, a heart of gold, fashionable, puking, dead as a doornail, obscene, bedazzled, addiction, faint-hearted, one fell swoop, vanish into thin air, swagger, zany, grovel, unreal, spotless reputation, full circle, arch-villain, bloodstained, all of a sudden.

121) Your purlicue is the skin connecting your fingers and thumb.

122) Cats have fallen from heights as great as 32 stories and survived. The cat who fell 32 stories had a chipped tooth and collapsed lung but went home two days after the fall. Researchers believe that cats instinctively know how to fall; for shorter falls, up to about seven

stories, cats don't reach terminal velocity and try to land feet first. For higher falls above seven stories where they reach terminal velocity, they splay their limbs out like a parachute and land on their belly increasing the chance of a collapsed lung or broken rib but greatly reducing the chance of a broken leg.

123) Portland, Oregon got its name when Asa Lovejoy and Francis Pettygrove flipped a coin in 1845. Lovejoy was from Massachusetts and wanted to name the new settlement Boston; Pettygrove was from Maine and wanted to name the new town Portland.

124) Thirteenth century Pope Gregory IX believed that black cats were an instrument of Satan; he condemned cats across Europe, and they were hunted down and killed.

125) At up to 10 feet long and 250 pounds, the Komodo dragon is the largest lizard in the world.

126) There is a basketball court one floor above the U.S. Supreme Court. It is named "The Highest Court in the Land" and was once a spare room to house journals. In the 1940s, it was converted into a workout area for courthouse workers, and backboards and baskets were installed later to create a smaller than regulation basketball court which is used by clerks, off-duty police officers, and other supreme court employees.

127) The Roman Empire at its peak was about 2.5 million square miles making it only the 19th largest empire by area in history.

128) President Bill Clinton lost the nuclear launch codes for months, and nobody found out. The president must keep the launch codes nearby, and every 30 days, a Pentagon staffer is required to check the codes to ensure they're correct, and the codes are replaced every four months. During one of these periods, the Pentagon staffer was told each time they came to check the codes that the president was too busy, and the staffer would leave. At the end of the fourth month, it became clear that Clinton had lost the codes. The procedure has since

been changed, and the Pentagon official must physically wait for as long as it takes to verify the codes.

129) A three-year study found that 54% of dog owners are willing to end a relationship if their dog doesn't like their partner, and 94% of dog owners consider their dogs to be a part of their family.

130) The banana is the world's largest herb plant with species growing up to 100 feet tall; it doesn't have a true woody trunk like a tree and behaves like a perennial.

131) In old age, human brains shrink by 10-15%; whereas, chimpanzees, our closest primate relatives, show no brain shrinkage with age. Researchers believe it may be due to extended longevity in humans which brain evolution hasn't kept up with.

132) The name Arctic is from the Greek word "Arktos" meaning bear; in this case, bear is a celestial reference to the Great and Little Bear constellations of the Northern Hemisphere. Antarctica comes from the Greek "Antarktikos" which means the opposite, and therefore, the opposite end of the Earth.

133) A desert locust swarm can cover 460 square miles and contain billions of locusts who can eat their own weight in plants each day consuming potentially hundreds of millions of pounds of vegetation per day.

134) An ultracrepidarian is a person who expresses opinions on matters outside the scope of their knowledge or expertise.

135) Because of its very high salt content, it is essentially impossible for a human to drown in the Dead Sea in the ordinary way. It is impossible for a human body to sink, but drownings have occurred when someone gets stuck on their stomach and can't get turned over. Experts recommend spending no more than 20 minutes at a time in the water to avoid dehydration and electrolyte imbalance from the high salt content.

136) Dire wolves, as seen in *Game of Thrones*, existed in the Americas up to about 10,000 years ago. They were about the same size as the largest modern gray wolves at about 150 pounds on average, but their teeth were larger with greater shearing ability, and they had the highest bite force of any known Canis species.

137) Medieval chastity belts are a myth; there is no credible evidence that they existed.

138) Abraham Lincoln and John F. Kennedy share some striking similarities although a century apart. Lincoln was elected to Congress in 1846; Kennedy was elected to Congress in 1946. Lincoln became President in 1860; Kennedy became president in 1960. Both were assassinated on a Friday and were sitting next to their wives when it happened, and both were succeeded after by a vice president named Johnson. Vice President Andrew Johnson was born in 1808; Vice President Lyndon Johnson was born in 1908.

139) Unconsciously, native English speakers say adjectives preceding nouns in a specific order: opinion, size, age, shape, color, origin, material, and purpose. That is why we say things instinctively like "big, old, black, leather chair" instead of "black, leather, old, big chair" which doesn't sound right.

140) Almost the entire continent of South America is east of the easternmost point of Florida. Mainland South America and Florida only overlap for a little more than one degree of longitude.

141) Despite her family ruling Egypt for about 270 years before her reign, Cleopatra was the first in her family to learn Egyptian.

142) For the longest recorded successful sniper shot of 2,475 meters, it took the bullet 6 seconds to reach its target.

143) If you wrote out every number in English (one, two, three, etc.), you wouldn't use the letter b until you reached one billion.

144) Samuel Morse, inventor of the telegraph, was an accomplished painter and didn't dedicate himself to improving long distance

communications until it took so long to get notified of his wife's illness that she was already dead and buried by the time he got home. Morse was working in Washington, D.C. on a painting commission when he received a letter from his father that his wife was gravely ill. He left immediately for his Connecticut home, but by the time he arrived, his wife had died and was already buried.

145) Nebraska is the only state that is at least three states or provinces away from the ocean in every direction.

146) Since 2016, it has been illegal in France for supermarkets to throw away edible food; they must donate it to charities.

147) People don't sneeze while they sleep because the brain shuts down the reflexes that would result in a sneeze through a process called REM atonia.

148) The common cold likely came from camels. Researchers have found that along with being the source of the Middle East Respiratory Syndrome (MERS) virus, camels are the likely source of the common cold which spread to humans thousands of years ago.

149) Unwinding a roll of Scotch tape can produce enough x-rays to image a finger. Flows of electrons are released as the tape is unpeeled and its adhesive snaps free of the surface. The electrical currents generate strong, short bursts of x-rays each about one billionth of a second long containing about 300,000 x-ray photons. Scientists were able to use the x-rays to image a finger. However, the phenomenon has been observed only when the tape is unpeeled in a vacuum.

150) Canada has more area devoted to national parks than any other country. There are over 145,000 square miles of national parks, an area larger than Norway.

151) Scottish scientist William Cullen invented and demonstrated the basis of modern refrigeration in 1748. He was able to boil diethyl ether to absorb heat from a space and cool it to the point that he could create ice. Refrigerators wouldn't enter the home until 1913.

152) In 1963, the United States launched 500 million whisker-thin copper wires into orbit to create a ring around the Earth in what was envisioned as the largest radio antenna ever and a way to protect long range communications if the Soviet Union attacked; it was called Project West Ford.

153) In Michigan, you are never more than six miles from a body of water. Michigan has over 11,000 inland lakes plus four of the five Great Lakes.

154) While Kodak didn't introduce color film to the masses until 1935, the first color photograph was taken in 1861. Thomas Sutton and James Clerk Maxwell created a picture of a Scottish tartan ribbon of red, white, and green. They created the photo by taking three separate photos using three different filters (red, green, and blue violet) and superimposing them together. This is the basic three-color method that is used in all color imaging to this day.

155) The avocado derives its name from the Nahuatl Indian word "āhuacatl" meaning testicle.

156) *The Addams Family* was the first television family with a computer in their home; they had a huge UNIVAC computer.

157) The U.S. President lives rent free at the White House, but they pay for personal and family meals, dry cleaning, hair, and makeup; the federal government pays for state dinners and other official functions.

158) America's first bank robbery occurred in August 1798 at the Bank of Pennsylvania in Philadelphia; the robbers got away with $162,821, and it resulted in a false imprisonment trial, a book, and the real robber depositing some of the stolen money back in the bank. Blacksmith Patrick Lyon became the primary suspect since he had recently installed new locks on the vault doors of the bank; he was arrested and eventually convicted. However, the real robbers were Thomas Cunningham and Isaac Davis. Cunningham was a porter at the bank and the inside man; he died of yellow fever soon after the robbery. Davis was caught after depositing stolen money at banks around

Philadelphia including the bank he robbed. However, he was given a pardon for making a full confession and returning the money and never spent any time in jail. Lyon served three months in prison before being released; he wrote a book about his experience and sued for wrongful imprisonment. It was one of the first trials in the U.S. to deal with the concept of probable cause, and he won $12,000 in damages.

159) The practice of using BC and AD for years wasn't established until the 6th century.

160) Since the end of WWII, Canada has instituted a policy where it has named thousands of its unnamed lakes after fallen soldiers from all three branches of the Canadian armed forces.

161) The sound of pain around the world differs. English speakers typically say "ouch!" or "aww!"; Spanish speakers usually say "uy!" or "ay!"; French speakers say "aïe!"; Germans say "aua!" or "autsch!"; Russians say "oi!"

162) Before electricity and gas lamps, it was common for people to wake in the middle of the night splitting their sleep into two periods. People would engage in different activities when they woke and then go back to sleep. People went to bed much earlier, and there was no prestige or value placed on staying up late by candlelight; even the wealthy who could afford candlelight felt there were better ways to spend their money.

163) On May 1, 1884, Moses Fleetwood Walker became the first African American to play Major League Baseball 63 years before Jackie Robinson's major league debut. He played 42 games for the Toledo Blue Stockings before suffering an injury and returning to the minor leagues. The Blue Stockings were formed as a minor league team in 1883 and moved to the major league for the 1884 season; they moved back to the minor leagues for the 1885 season which was their last season.

164) Lethologica is the word for when you can't remember a word.

165) Mississippi is the only state that doesn't have an open bottle law prohibiting drivers or passengers from drinking while driving. If the driver maintains a blood alcohol content below the 0.08% legal limit; it is legal to drink and drive.

166) Casu marzu is a traditional Sardinian sheep milk cheese that contains live maggots. The maggots are put into the cheese to promote fermentation and break down the cheese's fats. The cheese has a very soft texture, and the maggots appear as translucent white worms. Aficionados consider it unsafe to eat the cheese if the maggots in the cheese have died, so only cheese with living maggots is usually eaten.

167) A rat's front teeth grow 4½ to 5½ inches each year; like other rodents, they wear them down gnawing.

168) Only one side of the Moon is visible from Earth because the Moon rotates on its axis at the same rate that it orbits the Earth which is known as synchronous rotation, or tidal locking.

169) Nishiyama Onsen Keiunkan hotel in Yamanashi, Japan is the world's oldest hotel; it has been in operation since 705 and has been run by the same family for 52 generations. It has six natural hot springs baths and is on the edge of the Southern Japan Alps.

170) In the wild, there is no such thing as an alpha male wolf. Wolves act like families with the older members as leaders, so the leaders are simply parents. There's no fighting to move up the hierarchy, and they aren't born as leaders or followers.

171) In the 1830s, ketchup was sold as a cure for diarrhea, jaundice, indigestion, and rheumatism; they even made ketchup into pills. There had been a medical paper published in 1834 that claimed that tomatoes could treat digestive problems.

172) The manchineel tree which is native to tropical southern North America and northern South America is extremely toxic in all forms. Its milky white sap contains skin irritants which can cause blistering even

from standing beneath the tree during rain. Burning the tree can cause eye injuries, and the fruit is possibly fatal producing internal bleeding.

173) Studies have shown that the shape of an animal's eye pupil are evolutionary adaptations based on whether it's a predator or prey and how low to the ground the animal is. Circular pupils like humans tend to belong to predators; while rectangular pupils like a goat belong to grazing prey and provide a much wider field of vision to see predators. The rectangular pupils also allow them to take in more light without absorbing too much light from above their heads, so they can see the grass and their surroundings better. Grazing animals also rotate their eyes to keep their pupils nearly parallel to the ground when they lower their heads to feed. For predators, the proximity to the ground seems to dictate whether an animal has round or vertical pupils. Vertical pupils like snakes and small cats can expand much more than round pupils and provide more light for nocturnal activity and greater depth perception, but the advantages diminish as the animal gets further away from the ground which may be why larger cats and humans have round pupils.

174) The disclaimer that appears at the end of virtually every film that states the movie is a work of fiction and any similarity to actual persons living or dead or actual events is purely coincidental is due to Rasputin's murder. In the 1933 MGM film *Rasputin and the Empress*, Felix Yusupov, the man who assassinated Rasputin, and his wife Irina were portrayed under different names while they were both still alive. Since Felix had confessed to the killing, it was more difficult to prove a libel case around him, so Irina sued the studio for libel and won. Part of the problem for MGM was that they implied at the beginning of the film that it depicted real people and events. A justice in the case told MGM that the studio would have stood a better chance had they incorporated a disclaimer stating the opposite, so that is why the disclaimer exists on films today.

175) Researchers have found that most mammals weighing at least 6 pounds take about 21 seconds to urinate. The number seems to be quite

consistent with the urethra scaled to deliver about the same time regardless of the size of the animal.

176) The very first internet search engine was created in 1990 and was called Archie. The name stood for archive without the letter v and was created by a small group of computer science students at McGill University in Montreal, Quebec, Canada.

177) The Meganeura is the largest known flying insect to ever exist. It lived more than 300 million years ago during the Carboniferous Period and was a dragonfly-like insect with a wingspan of about 2.5 feet. It was a carnivore and fed on other insects and small amphibians.

178) *Alice's Adventures in Wonderland* was originally banned in China and other parts of the world because some people objected to the animal characters being able to use human language. They felt it wasn't right to put animals on the same level as humans.

179) Herbert Hoover was the first president born west of the Mississippi River; he was born in Iowa.

180) About 82% of the world's population has never flown on an airplane.

181) Mosquitos don't have teeth, but a mosquito's proboscis has 47 sharp edges on its tip to help it cut through skin and even clothing. The pain you feel when a mosquito bites is from the initial stab of sticking its proboscis into you.

182) If war is defined as an active conflict that has claimed more than 1,000 lives; humans have been entirely at peace for about 268 of the past 3,400 years or just 7.9% of the time.

183) A tornado can be nearly invisible. Since a tornado is just made up of wind, you don't see the tornado; what you see are the water droplets, dust, and debris that it picks up.

184) Actress Hedy Lamarr was also an inventor. At the beginning of World War II, she was involved in developing spread spectrum and

frequency hopping technology whose principles are incorporated into today's Bluetooth, CDMA, and Wi-Fi technologies.

185) Manatees are tropical animals and can suffer from cold stress if water temperatures fall below 68 degrees Fahrenheit.

186) *All in the Family*, *The Golden Girls*, and *Will & Grace* are the only three television series that won Emmys for all their main cast members.

187) Japanese railways have started installing shallow tunnels under the rail tracks to allow turtles to cross safely and avoid railway delays.

188) Scroop is the sound from the rustling of silk or similar cloth.

189) In the tiny Russian village of Tsovkra-1, every able person can walk a tightrope; the tradition began more than 100 years ago.

190) The Statue of Liberty is made of copper; about 62,000 pounds of copper were used to create it, and it looked like a new penny when it was first created.

191) Almost 96% of passengers involved in aviation accidents survive.

192) Via the longest continuous train route in the world, you can travel from Portugal to Vietnam covering over 10,700 miles and 17 countries in 13 days.

193) Insects only have one blood vessel; they have a single tube with the heart at one end and the aorta at the other which pumps blood to the brain. The blood flows back and fills all the spaces in the insect's body, so all the internal organs are floating in blood.

194) Dogs stare at you when they poop because they know they are vulnerable at that time, and they are looking to you, a member of their pack, for protection.

195) President John Quincy Adams believed that the Earth was hollow and signed off on an expedition to explore the empty core; the expedition never took place.

196) The poodle didn't originate in France; it is German. The name poodle came from the German pudel which means to "to splash about."

197) Snails are almost completely blind and don't have any mechanism to hear either, but their sense of smell is extraordinary.

198) From the late 1920s until the 1960s, Omero C. Catan became known as "Mr. First" in New York City because he made it his mission to participate in major firsts. He was the first person to board five different subway lines, first to dive into New York City's first public swimming pool, first ticket holder to enter two World's Fairs, first to skate at the Rockefeller Center ice rink, first to use the Brooklyn-Battery Tunnel, first to use the Lincoln Tunnel, first to feed a dime into the city's first parking meter, and many more. Catan went to great lengths to obtain his firsts waiting up to four days to gain a position or spending money to charter planes to be the first to land at both Idlewild (now JFK) and LaGuardia. In total, he ended up achieving 537 major firsts.

199) An adult blue whale's stomach can hold 2,200 pounds of krill at a time, and they require almost 9,000 pounds of krill a day.

200) There is a difference between coffins and caskets; coffins are typically tapered and six-sided; caskets are rectangular.

201) At the 1908 Olympics, dueling was a demonstration sport. It had two male competitors firing at each other with dueling pistols loaded with wax bullets. The competitors wore protective equipment for the torso, face, and hands.

202) Moray eels have two pairs of jaws. They have strong flesh tearing primary jaws that can cut through bone, and they have a pharyngeal jaw, a second pair of jaws located in their throat. When the eel captures prey with its primary jaws, it can use its secondary pharyngeal jaws to grab the prey and drag it down into its gullet for easy swallowing.

203) The shape of a Pringles chip is called a hyperbolic paraboloid; it allows easier stacking and reduces broken chips.

204) Oxford University existed about 350 years before the start of the Inca and Aztec empires. There was teaching at Oxford as early as 1076 making it the third oldest university in continuous operation in the world and the oldest English-speaking university. The Aztec and Incan empires weren't founded until the 1430s.

205) Australian Barry J. Marshall couldn't convince the scientific community that the H. pylori bacteria caused gastritis and stomach ulcers, so he drank the bacteria himself and developed gastritis within two weeks proving his theory. He went on to win the 2005 Nobel Prize in Physiology or Medicine for his work.

206) The United States borders three oceans - Atlantic, Pacific, and Arctic. Alaska's northern border is on the Arctic Ocean.

207) Sand dunes cover only about 15% of the Sahara Desert; rock plateaus and coarse gravel cover the majority.

208) Sixteenth century Danish astronomer, alchemist, and nobleman Tycho Brahe had a pet moose that liked to drink beer and died when it drank too much beer and fell down a flight of stairs.

209) It does snow occasionally in the Sahara Desert. There have been three recorded episodes of significant snowfall - February 1979, December 2016, and January 2018.

210) There are about 10,000 stars in the known universe for every grain of sand on Earth.

211) Human stomach acid is about as strong as battery acid and capable of destroying metal. Gastric acid consists of potassium chloride, sodium chloride, and hydrochloric acid, and on a PH scale of 0-14 with 0 being the most acidic and 7 being neutral, it typically measures between 1 and 3.

212) Demodex mites live on your face, and you're more likely to have them the older you get. They are sausage shaped with eight legs clustered in their front third; the largest are about one-third of a millimeter long. They spend most of their time buried head down in

your hair follicles; they're most commonly found in our eyelids, nose, cheeks, forehead, and chin. They like areas that have a lot of oils which is why they prefer the face. They can leave the hair follicles and slowly walk around on the skin especially at night, as they try to avoid light. The mites are transferred from person to person through contact with hair, eyebrows, and the sebaceous glands of the face. They eat, crawl, and reproduce on your face; the entire cycle from reproduction through death is about two weeks.

213) In 1804, Alexander Hamilton was shot and mortally wounded by Aaron Burr in a duel in the same location that his eldest son was shot and mortally wounded in a duel three years earlier in 1801.

214) The average garden snail has over 14,000 teeth which are arranged in rows on their tongue. The typical snail tongue might have 120 rows of 100 teeth; some species have more than 20,000 teeth.

215) The gender of most turtles, alligators, and crocodiles is determined after fertilization. The temperature of the eggs decides whether the offspring will be male or female; this is called temperature-dependent sex determination.

216) The Easter Island statues have full bodies not just heads. The remainder of the body is buried; the tallest statue excavated is 33 feet high.

217) In 1989, *Spy Magazine* sent out small checks to some of the wealthiest and most famous people to see who would cash them. They first sent out checks for $1.11 to 58 people; 26 people cashed them. They sent a second check for $0.64 to the 26 people who cashed the first check; 13 people cashed the second check. They sent a third check for $0.13 to the 13 people who cashed the second check; only 2 people, a Saudi Arabian arms dealer and Donald Trump, cashed the third check.

218) Outer space smells most like the burning odor of hydrocarbons like gunpowder, diesel, and barbecue. Astronauts have reported smelling burned or fried steak after a spacewalk.

219) Sharks have been around longer than trees. The first sharks appeared about 450 million years ago; the first trees were about 385 million years ago.

220) Dunce caps originally were a sign of intelligence. Thirteenth century philosopher John Duns Scotus created the idea of the pointy hat as a reverse funnel to spread knowledge into the brain; the hats became popular and a symbol of high intelligence. In the 1500s, Scotus' ideas fell out of favor, and the pointy hat eventually came to mean the opposite as we know it today.

221) If you are locked in a completely sealed room, you will die from carbon dioxide poisoning before you die from lack of oxygen.

222) Based on concerns that there were obscene lyrics inserted into the song, the FBI investigated the Kingsmen's 1963 version of "Louie Louie." In 1964, they abandoned the investigation after three months unable to discern what the lyrics were.

223) During WWII in Australia, Gunner, an Australian shepherd dog with extremely acute hearing, was able to warn air force personnel of incoming Japanese planes 20 minutes before they arrived. He could also differentiate allied and enemy aircraft.

224) At 8.1 square miles, Nauru in the South Pacific is the smallest island country.

225) Phosphenes are the rings or spots of light you see when you rub your eyes.

226) During the WWII Battle of Stalingrad, a railway station changed hands between German and Soviet control 14 times in one afternoon.

227) *The Wolf of Wall Street* used the "F" word more times (more than 500) than any other Best Picture Oscar nominee.

228) Before it was stolen from the Louvre in 1911, the *Mona Lisa* was not widely known outside the art world. Leonardo da Vinci painted it in 1507, but it wasn't until the 1860s that critics really noticed it as a

masterpiece. It wasn't even the most famous painting in its gallery at the Louvre let alone the entire Louvre.

229) Everyone that was alive when the oldest living person was born is dead.

230) Murmurations are the patterns starlings create when they flock together in the sky in swooping coordinated patterns.

231) Cats can drink saltwater and stay hydrated. Their kidneys are efficient enough to filter out the salt and use the water; humans can't.

232) Humans are the only animals with chins; scientists don't know why.

233) The toy company Mattel originally sold picture frames and later dollhouse furniture.

234) Hammerhead sharks are born with soft hammers bent back toward the tail to make it easier to give birth.

235) Strengths is the longest word in the English language with only one vowel.

236) Richard Nixon has been on the cover of *Time* magazine more times than any other person with 55 appearances.

237) The Centennial Light is the world's longest-lasting light bulb. It has burned since 1901 in Livermore, California.

238) Hawaii essentially has its own time zone. It is in the Hawaii-Aleutian Time Zone which includes Hawaii and Alaska's Aleutian Islands west of 169° 30' W longitude.

239) Dogs usually use their right ear when listening to other dogs, but they use their left ear when they hear threatening sounds.

240) A U.S. dollar bill only lasts about 18 months on average before it needs to be taken out of circulation and replaced.

241) In 1939, American author Ernest Vincent Wright published *Gadsby*, a 50,000-word novel that doesn't use the letter e.

242) The first video game console was the 1972 Magnavox Odyssey. It was five years before the first Atari and 13 years before the first Nintendo; it had no sound or color and came with 28 games including hockey, roulette, western shootout, and table tennis.

243) When the American Civil War started, Robert E. Lee didn't own any slaves, but Ulysses S. Grant did.

244) Prior to the early 1500s, the color we know as orange was called geoluhread in English meaning yellow-red. Orange wasn't used as a color in English until after the fruit was introduced to the British.

245) In Mozambique, human honey hunters work with wild birds known as honeyguides. The hunters use calls to bring out the honeyguides who find the hives in the cavities of baobabs and other tall trees. The humans break open the hives and take the honey and leave behind the wax and larvae for the honeyguides who are one of the few birds who can digest wax.

246) Sharks existed 200 million years before the dinosaurs and have changed relatively little.

247) The number zero with its own unique value and properties did not exist until the 7th century in India. Prior to that, early counting systems only saw zero as a placeholder, not a true number.

248) By slowing their heart rate, sloths can hold their breath for 40 minutes.

249) In protecting their hives from outsiders, bees will sometimes sting other bees.

250) Koala fingerprints are virtually indistinguishable from human fingerprints even with careful analysis under a microscope. They have the same loopy, whirling ridges as humans.

251) During WWII due to a lack of anti-tank weapons, the Soviet Union used dogs strapped with explosives against German tanks. The machine guns on German tanks were too high to reach the low-running suicide dogs, and the Germans couldn't easily emerge from their tanks and shoot the dogs since they were under fire. The dogs were trained to go under the tanks and helped destroy over 300 tanks during the war.

252) Sleep seems to clean the brain of harmful toxins. During sleep, the flow of cerebrospinal fluid in the brain increases dramatically washing away harmful waste proteins that build up in the brain during waking hours.

253) Matt Dillon who was played by James Arness on *Gunsmoke* from 1955 to 1975 and Detective John Munch who was played by Richard Belzer on *Homicide: Life on the Street* from 1993 to 1999 and on *Law & Order: Special Victims Unit* from 1999 to 2013 appeared for more consecutive years than any other male live action primetime characters on U.S. television.

254) In Switzerland, it is illegal to own just one guinea pig because they are social animals, and it is considered animal cruelty to deny them companionship.

255) At the age of 16, famous poet Maya Angelou was San Francisco's first African American female streetcar conductor.

256) On a per weight basis, spider silk has a tensile strength five times greater than steel. Each strand is 1,000 times thinner than a human hair and is made up of thousands of nanostrands only 20 millionths of a millimeter in diameter.

257) The Earth's continental plates drift about as fast as human fingernails grow.

258) Both male and female astronauts wear a maximum absorbency garment, an adult diaper with extra absorption material, during liftoff, landing, and extra-vehicular activity to absorb urine and feces. These

operations can take a long time or have significant delays, and astronauts can't just get up and go to the bathroom at any time.

259) The assassination of Archduke Franz Ferdinand of Austria in Sarajevo on June 28, 1914 is considered the event that initiated WWI; the assassination could have been avoided if the archduke's driver hadn't made a wrong turn. Ferdinand was visiting Sarajevo where seven potential assassins in favor of Bosnia and Herzegovina freedom from Austria-Hungary were scattered along his car route. One of the assassins threw a hand grenade at the archduke's open car, but it only wounded members of the archduke's entourage, and the remaining assassins didn't get a chance. Later the same day, the archduke decided to visit the hospital to see the men wounded in the grenade attack; his driver took a wrong turn on the way to the hospital, and while turning around, they came to a stop in front of a sidewalk cafe where one of the assassins, 19-year-old Gavrilo Princip, happened to be. Princip stepped out of the crowd and fired two shots from only about five feet away killing the archduke and his wife.

260) Different cells in the human body have very different lifespans. Sperm cells have a lifespan of about 3 days; colon cells die off after about 4 days; white blood cells live for about 13 days; cells in the top layer of your skin live about 30 days; red blood cells live for about 120 days, liver cells live about 18 months, and brain cells typically last an entire lifetime.

261) *Dune*, the bestselling science fiction book of all time, was rejected by more than 20 publishers before being published by Chilton Books, a little-known printing house best known for its auto repair manuals.

262) The footprints left behind by astronauts on the Moon could last 10 to 100 million years. The Moon has no atmosphere and consequently no wind or water to blow or wash anything away.

263) In space, the mucus that normally empties through your nose and drains down the throat backs up in the sinuses instead due to the lack of gravity. The only way to get rid of it is to blow into a tissue.

264) Charles Darwin ate many of the animal species he discovered.

265) In a study, the smell of Crayola crayons was among the top 20 smells most frequently identified. The unique smell is largely due to stearic acid which is a derivative of beef fat and is used to create the waxy consistency.

266) In 1964, grad student Donal Rusk Currey got his tree corer stuck in a bristlecone pine, and a park ranger helped him remove the tool by cutting the tree down. When Currey counted the rings, he found out the tree was almost 5,000 years old, the oldest ever recorded at that time.

267) The lunula is the white crescent near the base of your fingernail.

268) Ancient Rome had 24 hours in a day, but their hours varied in length based on the time of year. They ensured that there were 12 hours of daylight and 12 hours of darkness adjusting the length of the hours accordingly.

269) Santa Rita do Sapucai prison in Brazil allows prisoners to reduce their sentence by riding stationary bicycles to generate power for a nearby city. If they pedal for 16 hours, a prisoner's sentence is reduced by one day. The energy from the bikes charges batteries that are taken to the closest city.

270) At its triple point, a liquid can exist simultaneously as a liquid, solid, and gas. The triple point is the temperature and pressure that puts the three states of matter into thermodynamic equilibrium where no one state is trying to change into any other state. The boiling liquid causes high energy molecules to rise as a gas which lowers the temperature of the boiling liquid and makes it freeze. The cycle continues if the triple point temperature and pressure are maintained. For water, the triple point is at 32.02 degrees Fahrenheit and 0.006 atmospheres (normal pressure is one atmosphere).

271) In early Greece and Rome, it was essentially impossible to understand a text on a first reading. There was no punctuation or

spacing and no distinction between uppercase and lowercase letters; text was just a run on string of letters.

272) The highest fall that a person ever survived without a parachute is 33,330 feet due to an airplane explosion in 1972. The survivor spent several days in a coma and many months in the hospital but made an almost complete recovery.

273) One of the largest living things on Earth is Pando, a clonal colony of quaking aspen, that occupies 106 acres and weighs an estimated 6,600 tons in total with a single massive root system estimated to be 80,000 years old. A clonal colony is a group of genetically identical individuals that have grown in a given location from a single ancestor. Pando is in the Fishlake National Forest in Utah.

274) The first McDonald's drive-thru was created in 1975 in Sierra Vista, Arizona near the Fort Huachuca military base. It was designed to serve military personnel who weren't permitted to get out of their cars off base while wearing fatigues.

275) Against explicit orders, Portuguese diplomat Aristides de Sousa Mendes issued an estimated 30,000 Portuguese travel visas for Jewish families to flee persecution from the Nazis. He was stripped of his diplomatic position and forbidden from earning a living, and his 15 children were themselves blacklisted and prevented from attending university or finding meaningful work. He died in 1954, and the first recognition of his heroism didn't come until 1966 when Israel declared him to be a "Righteous Among the Nations." In 1986, the United States Congress also issued a proclamation honoring his heroic act.

276) All dogs are banned from Antarctica since 1994 because they might introduce diseases that could transfer to the native seals.

277) The original constitution of the United States included an open invitation for Canada to join the United States. Ratified in 1781, the Articles of Confederation were the original constitution of the United States which were replaced by the U.S. Constitution in 1789; there was a clause stating if Canada agreed to become a member of the United

States, they would automatically be accepted without the consent of the other states.

278) Fish yawn, cough, and burp.

279) Griffonage is careless handwriting, a crude or illegible scrawl.

280) Mosquitos are by far the deadliest animal in the world killing over 700,000 people worldwide annually primarily from malaria. Snakes are the second most deadly animal killing about 50,000 people; dogs are third at about 25,000 people mainly through rabies. Crocodiles are the biggest killer of the large animals at about 1,000 people worldwide; the hippopotamus is the world's deadliest large land mammal, killing an estimated 500 people per year.

281) Researchers locate penguin colonies by looking for the stain trail from their droppings via satellite. It is easier to see than looking for the penguins themselves.

282) The king of hearts is the only king in a standard card deck that doesn't have a mustache.

283) The cougar has more names than any other animal: puma, mountain lion, panther, catamount, or one of another 40 English, 18 native South American and 25 native North American names.

284) In the last century, the east coast of the United States has moved about eight feet further away from Europe.

285) President Herbert Hoover's physician invented a sport known as Hooverball to help keep the president fit. It is a combination of volleyball and tennis and is played with a six-pound medicine ball. The Hoover Presidential Library Association and the city of West Branch, Iowa still co-host a national Hooverball championship each year.

286) Pencils are typically yellow because that is the traditional color of Chinese royalty. In the 1890s when pencils started to be mass produced, the best graphite came from China, and manufacturers

wanted people to know they used the best quality graphite, so they painted them yellow, the color of Chinese royalty.

287) While the first usage of the word "selfie" didn't occur until 2002, the world's first known selfie was taken in 1839. Robert Cornelius took the first selfie inside his family's store in Philadelphia; he had to remove the camera's lens cap, run into frame, and hold his pose for a full minute.

288) After the fall of the Roman Empire, the technology to make concrete was lost for 1,000 years. Roman concrete is still more durable than the concrete we make today, and it gets stronger over time. Their concrete was created with volcanic ash, lime and seawater mixed with more volcanic rock as aggregate which created a rock like concrete we haven't been able to duplicate.

289) Karl Marx was once a foreign correspondent for Horace Greeley's *New York Daily Tribune* newspaper.

290) The youngest signer of the United States Declaration of Independence was Edward Rutledge who was a lawyer from South Carolina and was only 26 at the time. Benjamin Franklin was the oldest signer at 70.

291) SOS doesn't stand for "save our ship" or anything else; it was selected as a distress signal because it is easy to transmit – three dots, three dashes, three dots.

292) In the interests of her own or her son's future rule, Cleopatra likely had a hand in the deaths of both of her sibling husbands and in the execution of her sister.

293) In some circumstances, female dragonflies fake death to avoid mating. The process is called sexual death feigning where a female dragonfly will drop to the ground as if dead to avoid an overly aggressive male. Scientists found that it worked about 60% of the time.

294) Without saliva, you wouldn't be able to taste your food. Enzymes in your saliva break down the food and release molecules that are picked up by your taste buds.

295) If California was a country, it would have the 8th largest economy in the world.

296) The sound you hear when you hold a seashell to your ear is surrounding environmental noise resonating in the seashell cavity. In a soundproof room, you don't hear anything when you hold a seashell to your ear.

297) Barcelona, Spain has hundreds of playgrounds for seniors which are designed to promote physical fitness and provide social interaction.

298) The difference between antlers (found on deer, elk, moose) and horns (found on pronghorn antelope, bighorn sheep, bison) is that antlers are an extension of the animal's skull, and they are true bone and shed and regrown each year. Horns are composed of an interior bone that is an extension of the skull covered by an exterior sheath grown by specialized hair follicles like your fingernails, and they aren't shed and continue to grow throughout the animal's life. The exception is the pronghorn antelope which sheds and regrows its horn sheath each year.

299) The liver is the only human internal organ that can regenerate itself. You can lose up to 75% of your liver, and the remaining portion can regenerate into a whole liver. Therefore, living donor liver transplants can be done where a portion of the liver is taken, and both the donor and recipient's portion regrows into a full liver within about four months. A liver from a deceased donor may also be split and transplanted into two recipients.

300) The technical term for a cat's hairball is bezoar. The term also applies to a mass of indigestible material found in the gastrointestinal tract of other animals including humans.

# Facts 301-600

301) Alien hand syndrome or sometimes called Dr. Strangelove syndrome is a condition where a person's limb acts seemingly on its own without control. It can be caused by separation of the brain hemispheres and most frequently affects the left hand.

302) Cellophane was invented in 1908 as a cloth to repel liquids rather than absorb them after the inventor saw wine spilled on a tablecloth.

303) In ancient Egypt, people put a dead mouse cut in half in their mouth to cure a toothache.

304) Red is the rarest human hair color with less than 2% of the world's population.

305) The television sitcom *Happy Days* originated the term "jumped the shark" for when a show takes a sharp drop in quality or has inserted desperate attempts for ratings. During the season five opening episode, Fonzie jumped a shark while water skiing which marked the beginning of a sharp decline in the show's quality.

306) Human testicles hang outside the body because sperm dies at body temperature.

307) About 20% of the world's households don't have a television.

308) A fire rainbow looks like a rainbow in the clouds, but it is technically called a circumhorizontal arc. It occurs when the sun is higher than 58° above the horizon and its light passes through high-altitude cirrus clouds made up of hexagonal plate ice crystals. When aligned properly, the ice crystals act as a prism, resulting in refraction that looks like a rainbow in the clouds.

309) Monowi, Nebraska is the only incorporated town in the U.S. with a population of one. Elsie Eiler, its lone resident, used to live there with her husband until he passed away in 2004. She is the mayor, bartender,

and librarian and is responsible for paying herself taxes and granting herself a liquor license.

310) A ship's speed is measured in knots because they historically used real knots to measure speed. By the late 16th century, sailors measured a ship's speed by throwing out a piece of wood attached to a length of rope with knots tied at regular intervals; they allowed the rope to go out as the ship moved forward, and after a set length of time, they pulled the rope back in counting the knots that had gone out and calculated the speed. A knot eventually came to mean one nautical mile per hour.

311) Dental drilling dates back at least 9,000 years. Ancient dentists drilled nearly perfect holes as early as 7,000 BC.

312) Alfred Nobel made his money to establish the Nobel Prizes through his invention of dynamite; he wanted to make up for all the destruction his invention had caused.

313) The word "computer" is referenced as far back as the early 1600s, but it originally meant a person who did arithmetic calculations. It didn't take on its meaning of being a machine until the late 1800s and an electronic device until the mid-1900s.

314) The name IKEA is formed from the founder Ingvar Kamprad's initials (IK) plus the first letters of Elmtaryd (E) and Agunnaryd (A) from the farm and village where he grew up.

315) The 1900 Paris Olympics had long jump and high jump competitions for horses. The winning long jump was 6.10 meters; the winning high jump was 1.85 meters.

316) Although the triggering mechanism is different, dead people can get goosebumps. As rigor mortis sets in, muscles contract and the arrector pili muscles attached to the hair follicles also contract producing goosebumps.

317) You can get all the way from Norway to North Korea by land going through just one country - Russia.

318) The letter j was the last letter added to the English alphabet. The letters i and j were treated the same for a long time until Italian Gian Giorgio Trissino made the distinction between them in 1525; j finally entered the alphabet in the 19th century.

319) The word "robot" was first used in a 1920 play called *Rossum's Universal Robots* by Czech writer Karel Čapek. It comes from the Slavic word "rabota" meaning slave labor.

320) Studies have shown that people over 60 have a 14% higher chance of dying on their birthday than on any other day. Due to increased stress on birthdays, heart attacks, strokes, falls, and suicides are all more likely.

321) Major league baseball umpires are required to wear black underwear in case their pants split.

322) Humans have a gaze detection system that is especially sensitive to whether someone is looking directly at you or whether their gaze is averted just a few degrees. Studies have recorded brain activity and found that specific brain cells fire when the gaze is direct; others fire if the gaze is just a few degrees off. Our brain specialization is an indication how important eye contact is when communicating with others

323) Women in 16th century France could sue their husbands for erectile dysfunction. The trials could involve examinations of the genitals to prove that the man could achieve erection or even evidence that the couple could consummate their marriage by forcing a husband and wife to have sex in front of witnesses. Divorce was largely forbidden, but it was viewed as a marital responsibility to be able to produce children, so if a man could not, it was viewed as an act against religion and a reason to re-evaluate the marriage.

324) The X in airport code names is usually just a filler. Airports typically used the two letter codes that the National Weather Service used for cities; when the three-letter code was made standard, some airports simply added the X to comply, thus LAX, PDX, etc.

325) Diomede Islands in the Aleutians are made up of two islands separated by 2.4 miles, owned by two different countries, and have a 21-hour time difference between them. One is owned by Russia, and the other is owned by the United States; they represent the closest distance between the two countries, but the time difference is 21 hours due to the international date line passing between the islands.

326) Chameleons don't change their colors for camouflage purposes. They change color by stretching and relaxing cells that contain crystals which affects how the light is reflected, but their primary purposes for changing color are to communicate with other chameleons (dark colors signal aggression) and to regulate their temperature (lighter colors reflect the heat).

327) Paper cuts hurt more than other cuts for a combination of reasons. They most often occur in the tips of the fingers which have more pain receptors than almost anywhere else in the body, and paper edges also aren't as smooth as they appear and can leave a rough cut. Finally, paper cuts aren't deep enough to trigger some of the body's defense mechanisms like blood clotting and scabbing, so the damaged nerve endings remain exposed.

328) The average American home has 300,000 things in it.

329) There are so many possible sequences when you shuffle a deck of 52 cards that it is statistically likely that a well shuffled deck is in a sequence that has never occurred before and will never occur again. There are $8.07 \times 10^{67}$ possible sequences for a deck of 52 cards; there are only about $10^{24}$ stars in the observable universe.

330) Female cats are significantly more likely to be right paw dominant, and male cats typically favor their left paw. Cats don't seem to have an overall preference for right or left as humans do, and researchers theorize their preferences are linked to neural differences.

331) Mushrooms are more closely related to humans than they are to plants. Animals and fungi branched off from plants about 1.1 billion

years ago; later, animals and fungi separated genealogically making mushrooms closer to humans than to plants.

332) The brand name WD-40 literally stands for Water Displacement, 40th formula. The chemist who developed it was trying to create a product to prevent corrosion which is done by displacing water.

333) President John Quincy Adams often swam in the Potomac River and preferred to do it in the buff. He wrote of waking at about 4 am and taking a nude morning dip.

334) The longest recorded time a chicken has flown continuously is 13 seconds. The longest distance chicken flight ever recorded is 301.5 feet.

335) The Earth's surface curves out of sight at about 3.1 miles.

336) Studies have shown that male rhesus macaque monkeys will pay to look at pictures of a female monkey's bottom. The male monkeys were willing to give up their juice rewards in order to look at the pictures, so it is akin to paying to look at images. They would also pay to look at images of high ranking or powerful monkeys just like people look at famous or powerful people.

337) Venus rotates so slowly that you could watch a sunset forever just by walking towards it. At the equator, Venus rotates 4 mph; the Earth rotates 1,038 mph at the equator.

338) In a process known as "cuddle death" or "balling" when the queen of a bee colony becomes too old or unproductive, the worker bees dispose of her by clustering around her in a tight ball until she overheats and dies.

339) There are multiple times more deaths caused by taking selfies each year than there are by shark attacks.

340) Abstemious and facetious are the only two words in the English language that have all five vowels in order.

341) To avoid dating relatives, Iceland has a phone app that lets users bump phones to see if they are related. Iceland has a relatively small

population of over 300,000 people and is somewhat insular, so most people are distantly related. The app emits a warning alarm if people are closely related, so they know not to date.

342) Alcatraz used to be the only U.S. federal prison where inmates got hot showers. They didn't want inmates to get acclimatized to cold water in case they tried to swim to shore.

343) The average human body worldwide has a volume of about 2.22 cubic feet.

344) The giant clam is the largest mollusk and can reach 4 feet in length and weigh more than 500 pounds. They live in the warm waters of the South Pacific and Indian Oceans and can live more than 100 years.

345) In 1912, a Paris foundling hospital held a raffle of live babies to raise money and find homes for orphaned children. The management of the hospital held the raffle with the consent of authorities; the raffle proceeds were divided among several charities.

346) Platypuses sweat milk. They secrete milk from mammary glands like other mammals, but they don't have nipples, so the milk oozes from the surface of their skin more like sweat. Because the delivery system is less hygienic, platypus milk contains antibacterial proteins to protect the babies.

347) Until 1953, New York City had a pneumatic tube mail network that spanned 27 miles and connected 23 post offices. At its peak, the system moved 95,000 letters a day at speeds of 30-35 mph.

348) Horseshoe crabs have 10 eyes spread all over their body; they have eyes on top of their shell, on their tail, and near their mouth.

349) Coca-Cola didn't entirely remove cocaine as an ingredient until 1929. Most of the cocaine had been eliminated in 1903.

350) In 1797, John Hetherington, who is often credited with inventing the top hat, caused a riot when he first wore it in public. He was

charged with breaching the king's peace and ordered to pay a 50 pound fine. People had never seen a top hat before and were scared and started rioting.

351) The first television sitcom in the world was *Pinwright's Progress* which debuted on November 29, 1946 on the BBC. it featured the adventures of the smallest store in the world and included the store proprietor, his pretty daughter, a nemesis, and helpful staff who end up making things worse.

352) There is a very rare third type of human twin called sesquizygous or semi-identical. Identical or monozygotic twins result from a single fertilized egg that splits in two and forms two identical boys or two identical girls who share 100% of their DNA. Fraternal or dizygotic twins form from two eggs that have been fertilized by two of the father's sperm creating two genetically unique siblings that share 50% of their DNA. Semi-identical twins are so rare that only two cases have ever been identified; they share between 50% and 100% of their DNA and are formed when a single egg is fertilized by two sperm. This shouldn't happen because once a sperm enters the egg, the egg locks down to prevent another sperm from entering. Even if a second sperm entered, an embryo with three rather than the normal two sets of chromosomes won't survive. To produce semi-identical twins, the egg splits the three sets of chromosomes into two separate cell sets.

353) On the day he was shot at Ford's Theatre, Abraham Lincoln signed legislation creating the U.S. Secret Service. The original mission of the Secret Service was solely to combat currency counterfeiting; it wasn't until 1901 after the killing of two more presidents that it was also tasked with protecting the president.

354) A googleganger is a person with the same name who shows up in results when you Google yourself.

355) Pantheism is the belief that the universe as a whole is God.

356) The term genuine leather means that the product is made of real leather, but it also means it is the lowest quality of all products made from real leather.

357) Woolsey Hall auditorium at Yale University still has an extra wide seat built for William Howard Taft. After his presidency, Taft went on to teach at Yale which installed several special chairs with extra-wide seats to accommodate Taft who was well over 300 pounds. One of the chairs is still in use in Woolsey Hall today; it is balcony seat E-9.

358) Writer T.S. Eliot wore green makeup; no one is quite sure why he dusted his face with green powder, but some speculate he was just trying to look more interesting.

359) Crayola means oily chalk. It combines the French word "craie" meaning chalk with "ola", shortened from the French word "oléagineux" meaning oily.

360) If they are swimming near each other, alligators will always give manatees the right of way.

361) If your mind believes that an object is further away based on visual clues, it assumes it is larger even if it is the same size as an object that appears to be nearer. This is known as the Ponzo illusion which was first demonstrated in 1911 by the Italian psychologist Mario Ponzo who suggested that the human mind judges an object's size based on its background.

362) Due to the loss of players to military service in WWII, the NFL Pittsburgh Steelers and Philadelphia Eagles were forced to merge for the 1943 season to form the Steagles. The official record books list the combined team as the Phil-Pitt Combine.

363) At its peak, the British Empire was the largest empire by area in history; in 1922, it ruled over about 24% of the world's land.

364) The current population of Ireland (Northern Ireland and Ireland) is still about 20% less than it was before the great potato famine started in 1845.

365) In ancient Greece, women would go to great lengths to have a thick, swarthy unibrow. To the Greeks, a unibrow signaled beauty and brains; women would line their brows with soot or use tree resin to attach fake eyebrows made of goat hair to their foreheads.

366) Worldwide, more than 10% of marriages are between first or second cousins.

367) In the human body, there are about 200 different kinds of cells, and within those cells, there are about 20 different kinds of structures.

368) When Disneyland opened in 1955, Tomorrowland was designed to look like 1986, the distant future.

369) When you read to yourself, your tongue and vocal cords still get movement signals from the brain. The process is known as subvocal speech and is characterized by minuscule movements in the larynx and other muscles involved in the articulation of speech; the movements are undetectable without the aid of machines.

370) Technically, United States Independence Day is July 2, 1776 which is when Congress voted America free from British rule. July 4 is the day the Declaration of Independence was adopted.

371) Crapulous is the feeling you get from eating or drinking too much.

372) The medical name for the human butt crack is the intergluteal cleft.

373) King Louis XIV of France is the longest reigning monarch ever at 72 years, 110 days from 1643-1715.

374) Caterpillars essentially dissolve themselves to become butterflies. In the cocoon, the caterpillar releases enzymes to dissolve all its tissues. It then begins rapid cell division to form the features of an adult butterfly or moth.

375) Ravens, crows, jays, and some songbirds lie in anthills and roll around letting the ants swarm on them, or they chew up the ants and

rub them on their feathers. It is called anting, and it isn't understood why they do it.

376) Mapmakers have a long tradition of putting slight inaccuracies in their maps to catch people who may try to copy their work. Typically, it is something small like a nonexistent dead end, fake river bend, or adjusted mountain elevation. However, in one case, a mapmaker put in the fictional town of Agloe, New York. When a store was built in the corresponding location, the owner read the map and named it Agloe General Store assuming that was a real area name, so a fictional location became real.

377) At the Palace of Versailles, there were no restrooms, so people would just defecate in the corners. Visitors often complained about how bad the palace smelled, and King Louis XIV ordered that the hallways be cleaned of feces at least once a week, and they brought in orange trees planted in vases to mask the smell.

378) On average, a person grows 450 miles of hair on their head over their lifetime.

379) The Amazon rainforest produces more than 20% of the world's oxygen.

380) During a typical lifetime, people spend about six years dreaming.

381) *The Simpsons* has been the longest running primetime scripted show on U.S. television longer than any other show in history; it has been the longest running show since July 1998.

382) Ancient Greek men didn't wear trousers; they thought men from other cultures who wore them were barbaric and effeminate.

383) The force required to topple a domino is less than the force it generates when it falls; this force amplification can be used to topple ever larger dominos. Each domino can be about 1.5 times larger than the preceding one. Starting with a regular size domino at about 1.875 inches tall and pushing it over, the 25th domino toppled would be

about 2,630 feet tall, about the height of the tallest building in the world.

384) Your right ear is better at receiving sounds from speech, and your left ear is more sensitive to sounds of music.

385) The Andes are the longest above-water mountain range in the world at 4,300 miles, but the mid-ocean ridge at 25,097 miles is the longest if you include underwater ranges. The mid-ocean ridges of all the world's oceans are connected.

386) Lobsters have urine release nozzles right under their eyes, and they urinate as a way of communicating with each other.

387) Dogs normally start sniffing with their right nostril and keep using the right nostril if the smell is something unpleasant or potentially dangerous. If the smell is something pleasant, they will switch to use their left nostril.

388) The Etruscan shrew is the smallest mammal by mass weighing about 0.06 ounces on average. The shrew has a very fast metabolism and eats 1.5 to 2 times its own body weight per day. It also has the fastest heartbeat of any mammal at 1,500 beats per minute.

389) Eye floaters are those tiny spots, specks, or cobwebs that drift around in your field of vision. Most eye floaters are caused by age-related changes that occur as the jelly-like substance inside your eyes becomes more liquid. Microscopic fibers within the eye clump and can cast tiny shadows on your retina; what you see are the shadows and not the floaters themselves.

390) Male pandas perform a handstand when they urinate. By doing the handstand, they get their pee higher up the tree allowing their scent to be carried further and increasing their mating chances.

391) The Bible doesn't say Adam and Eve ate an apple. It says they ate the forbidden fruit from the tree of knowledge; nowhere does it say it was an apple.

392) Oscar winning actor J.K. Simmons has been the voice of the Yellow Peanut M&M since the late 1990s.

393) Reindeer eyes change color from gold in summer to blue in winter. During bright summer light, their eyes reflect most light and look gold; during winter, the tissue behind their retina becomes less reflective, and their eyes appear blue. This increases their light sensitivity and vision in the low winter light.

394) In the early 19th century, some of the most stylish men in London and Paris polished their shoes with champagne. Beau Brummell, the preeminent example of an English dandy of that time, swore by the method to make his shoes the blackest black.

395) All the gold ever mined in the history of the world would fit in a 67-foot cube.

396) The world's largest recorded turtle was a leatherback turtle that washed up on Harlech Beach, Wales in 1988. It was estimated to be 100 years old and was almost 9 feet long and weighed 2,016 pounds.

397) Even though Froot Loops cereal has a variety of colors, all colors have the same flavor, a fruit blend.

398) Over the last 20,000 years, the size of the average human brain has shrunk by about 10%. There are no clear answers why.

399) Pablo Picasso's full name was Pablo Diego José Francisco de Paula Juan Nepomuceno María de los Remedios Cipriano de la Santísima Trinidad Ruiz y Picasso.

400) Due to spinal decompression while you are sleeping, you are about one centimeter taller when you wake up in the morning.

401) Dysania is the state of finding it hard to get out of bed in the morning.

402) Apple founder Steve Jobs was adopted at birth; later in life, he decided to find his biological family. He found his mother and sister, and his sister found their father who was a Syrian immigrant and

owned a restaurant in California. When his sister went to meet their father, Jobs asked her not to mention anything about him. When talking to her father, he mentioned that famous people came to his restaurant and mentioned Steve Jobs as one of them. When his sister told Jobs of this, he remembered meeting the restaurant owner multiple times. The two never met in person after knowing who each other was.

403) $1.19 (three quarters, four dimes and four pennies) is the most money you can have in change and not be able to make change for a dollar.

404) Victoria's Secret was originally created to be a store where men could feel comfortable buying lingerie for their female partner. The founder was embarrassed years earlier buying lingerie for his wife at a department store where he felt like an intruder and wanted to change that.

405) Every Dutch police car is equipped with a teddy bear in case they need to comfort a child during a traumatic experience.

406) An aphthong is a letter or combination of letters in a word that are not pronounced. The "gh" combination in the word night is an aphthong.

407) Despite what you see in the movies, Roman warships were not rowed by slaves. Only free Roman citizens had a duty to fight for the state; in exceptional times if they needed more men, they would admit slaves to the military, but they were either freed before enlisting or promised freedom if they fought well.

408) An autological word is a word that describes itself; some examples include word, noun, polysyllabic, unhyphenated, suffixed.

409) Ravens can learn to talk better than some parrots, and they also mimic other noises including other animals and birds. They have even been known to imitate wolves or foxes to attract them to a carcass to break it open, so the raven can get at it when they are done.

410) Neanderthals mass produced thousands of flint tools in a huge workshop 60,000 years ago. Archaeologists in Poland recovered 17,000 stone products from the site which was not in a cave.

411) A male dog lifts his leg to pee because he wants to leave his mark as high as possible as a sign of size and status. He also prefers to pee on vertical objects because the scent lasts longer.

412) Before clocks, there were candle clocks which showed the passage of time by how far a candle burned. They could even be turned into an alarm clock of sorts by pushing a nail in at the desired point; the nail would fall and clank when the candle burned down to that point.

413) William Howard Taft was the first president to throw out a first pitch at an MLB game in 1910.

414) President Richard Nixon was an accomplished musician and could play five instruments – piano, saxophone, clarinet, accordion, and violin – and did so frequently.

415) Pepperoni is an American creation of the early 20th century.

416) Ironically, dentists helped popularize cotton candy. Machine spun cotton candy was invented by John C. Wharton, a candy maker, and William Morrison, a dentist, in 1897. They called it fairy floss and sold thousands of servings at the St. Louis World's Fair in 1904. Joseph Lascaux, a dentist, patented another machine in 1921 and was the first to use the name cotton candy.

417) The farthest object visible to the naked human eye is the Andromeda Galaxy 2.6 million light-years away. It is visible as a dim, large gray cloud almost directly overhead in a clear night sky.

418) WWI greatly increased the number of women wearing bras. Before the war, corsets were still the norm, but corset frames were mostly made of metal, which was needed for the war effort, so the U.S. War Industries Board asked American women in 1917 to stop buying them accelerating the move to bras.

419) Toilet paper traces its origins to at least 6th century China when it was first referenced in writings. Most people didn't use toilet paper until at least 1857 when American inventor Joseph Gayetty commercialized the product much as we know it today.

420) The small bump on the inner corner of your eye is the caruncula.

421) The term Nazi existed prior to Hitler and was associated with backwards peasants. The term was popularized by Hitler's opponents, and it was rarely used and disliked by the Nazis.

422) Urohidrosis is the habit of some birds of defecating onto their legs and feet to cool themselves. For birds, solid and liquid wastes are expelled together, so it is a liquid mixture of feces and urine. Flamingos, several species of storks, and some vultures exhibit this behavior.

423) The state name Idaho was proposed by a lobbyist who claimed it was a Shoshone word meaning "Gem of the Mountains"; in reality, he just made it up.

424) In *Star Wars Episode V: The Empire Strikes Back*, Darth Vader never says, "Luke, I am your father." Instead, he says, "No, I am your father."

425) You can't hum while holding your nose; air must escape through your nose to create the humming sound.

426) Its purpose isn't known, but about 39% of the population has a bone in their knee called the fabella. From historical studies, the percentage fell from 17% in 1875 to 11% in 1918 before rising to the current number.

427) In the 18th and 19th centuries, squirrels were popular pets. They were sold in pet shops and were a preferred pet among the wealthy.

428) President Ulysses S. Grant was arrested and taken into custody for speeding with a horse and buggy in Washington D.C. while he was in

office. The police seized his horse and buggy, and he paid a fine and walked back to the White House.

429) Early humans in South America hunted giant armadillos that were about the size and weight of a Volkswagen Beetle; they used their shells for homes.

430) A female rat can mate as many as 500 times during a six-hour period and can do that about 15 times per year.

431) The Pilgrims didn't first land at Plymouth Rock; they first landed in what is now Provincetown, Massachusetts and signed the Mayflower Compact there. They arrived at Plymouth Rock five weeks later.

432) During the 1960s, Canada employed what was known as a fruit machine that was supposed to be able to identify gay men. The subjects viewed naked or semi-naked images of men and women, and the device measured their pupil response to see if the pupil enlarged as an indication of attraction. It was employed as part of a campaign to eliminate all gay men from the civil service, the Royal Canadian Mounted Police, and the military; although the device didn't work, a substantial number of workers did lose their jobs. Funding for the project was discontinued in 1967.

433) In 1974, the *Journal of Applied Behavior Analysis* published a paper titled "The Unsuccessful Self-Treatment of a Case of Writer's Block"; it contained no words.

434) Diarrhea is the second leading cause of death among children under the age of five; it kills more children than AIDS, malaria, and measles combined.

435) Due to a metal shortage during WWII, Oscars were made of painted plaster for three years. Following the war, the Academy invited recipients to trade in their plaster awards for normal gold-plated metal statuettes.

436) President John Quincy Adams kept a journal from the age of 12 until just before his death; it totaled 51 volumes and 14,000 pages.

437) Only 5% of the universe is made up of normal matter; 25% is composed of dark matter; 70% is dark energy.

438) The state of Virginia extends further west than West Virginia.

439) Junk email is called spam because of Monty Python. The 1970 *Monty Python's Flying Circus* sketch where a waitress reads a menu with an endless variety of Spam options and a chorus of Vikings sings "Spam, Spam, Spam, Spam" resulted in spam being used generically for something that drowns out or overrides everything else like junk email does.

440) In the 15th century, King Louis XI of France ordered Abbot de Beigne to create a musical instrument using the voices of pigs. He built a keyboard which jabbed a spike into the rumps of pigs to produce a squeal. A similar instrument was designed in Cincinnati 400 years later.

441) Uranus was originally called Planet George in honor of English King George III.

442) Sideburns are named after American Civil War general Ambrose Burnside who was known for having an unusual facial hairstyle with a moustache connected to thick sideburns with a clean-shaven chin.

443) The stage before frostbite is called frostnip where there is skin irritation causing redness and cold feeling followed by numbness, but there is no permanent damage.

444) If you wanted to dig a hole straight through the center of the Earth and end up in China, you would have to start in Argentina.

445) With two exceptions, China owns all the giant pandas in the world. Any panda in a foreign zoo is on loan from China with the agreement that China owns the panda and any offspring which must be returned to China before they are four years old. The only exceptions are two pandas China gave to Mexico prior to implementing the current policy.

446) Every second, the Sun produces as much energy as over 90 billion one-megaton nuclear bombs.

447) Nerve signals in the human body travel at different speeds depending on the type of impulse. Muscle position impulses travel at speeds up to 266 mph; pain signals travel much slower at only 1.4 mph; touch signals travel at 170 mph. You feel the touch that produces the pain 2-3 seconds before you feel the associated pain.

448) McDonald's uses over 10% of the potatoes harvested in the U.S. annually.

449) Natural redheads require about 20% more anesthesia to be sedated and require more topical anesthetics, but they need lower doses of pain killers like opioids. They also seem to be less sensitive to electric shock, needle pricks, and stinging pain. Both parents must pass along a recessive trait for their child to have red hair. The trait is also responsible for skin color and for midbrain function that determines pain response.

450) The first artificial intelligence generated research book was published in 2019 by an author named Beta Writer. The algorithm was designed by researchers from Goethe University in Frankfurt, Germany. The book is about the state of current research on lithium-ion batteries.

451) Melanistic animals are the opposite of albinos. They are all black instead of all white and have an excess of melanin that makes their skin, hair, or fur very dark or black.

452) The sign we know as the ampersand (&) was the 27th letter of the English alphabet before being dropped. It wasn't called an ampersand at that time and was referred to as "and."

453) A group of hippos is called a bloat.

454) Zambia has a larger percent of its area devoted to national parks than any other country; national parks make up 32% of its area.

455) Sound travels over four times faster in water than it does in air.

456) Warren Buffett, one of the richest men in the world, stops at McDonald's every morning on his way to the office for breakfast. He always spends between $2.61 and $3.17 on breakfast. He gets either two sausage patties and a Coke for $2.61, a sausage, egg and cheese for $2.95, or a bacon, egg and cheese biscuit for $3.17 depending on how he feels about things. He tells his wife each morning while he shaves what option he wants for that day, and she puts the exact change in his car.

457) Albert Einstein is an anagram for "ten elite brains."

458) If you go north, south, east, or west from Stamford, Connecticut, the next state you hit is New York.

459) Jiffy is an actual measured unit of time. It has been used for different time values in different fields; in computer science, a jiffy defines the duration of one tick of a timer interrupt, usually 1-10 milliseconds. It also was defined as the time between electrical alternating current cycles. Today, it typically means 0.01 seconds.

460) Fish odor syndrome is a genetic disease characterized by an offensive body odor and the smell of rotting fish due to the excessive excretion of trimethylaminuria (TMA) in the urine, sweat, and breath of those affected.

461) The Great Pyramid of Giza was originally covered in highly polished white limestone; it was removed over time to be used for other building projects.

462) *Law & Order: Special Victims Unit* is the longest running spinoff in the history of American television; it debuted in 1999.

463) At 142 feet in diameter, the Roman Pantheon's dome is still the largest unreinforced concrete dome in the world; it was built in 125 AD.

464) With about 127 million people, Japan rarely sees more than 10 gun deaths per year. That is lower than your chance of getting killed by lightning in the United States.

465) It is illegal to take pictures of the Eiffel Tower at night. French copyright law gives the original creator of an object exclusive rights to its sale and distribution; this includes buildings and lasts for 70 years after death. Gustave Eiffel, the tower creator, died in 1923 which means the copyright ran out in 1993 making the likeness and design public domain at that point. The Las Vegas replica wasn't built until 1999. Night photos are still protected by copyright because the Eiffel Tower lights were installed in 1985 and are considered a separate artistic work by their creator Pierre Bideau and protected by copyright until 70 years after his death.

466) Interracial marriage wasn't fully legal in all U.S. states until 1967, so it was banned in some form for 191 years. It was only banned in South Africa for 36 years from 1949 to 1985.

467) Millions of Japanese treat themselves to KFC chicken every Christmas. In 1974, KFC created a national marketing campaign "Kentucky for Christmas"; it became so popular that Christmas KFC sales can be 10 times the normal sales volume. Christmas dinner often requires ordering weeks in advance or waiting in line for hours. There was no real Christmas tradition in Japan prior to the original advertising campaign, so KFC was able to establish themselves as a tradition of their own.

468) Constantinople was one of the largest and wealthiest cities in Europe from the mid-5th to the early 13th century; it had survived many attacks and sieges and was regarded as one of the most impregnable cities with an outer ditch and three rings of walls. In 1453, the city was besieged by the Turks and someone accidentally left one of the small gates open allowing the Turks to get in. The city may have fallen regardless, but the open gate quickened its demise. The inhabitants were killed or enslaved, and Emperor Constantine XI was killed.

469) In South Korea, there is an emergency phone number to report spies; it is 113.

470) In 1958, a B-47 carrying an atomic bomb larger than the one dropped on Nagasaki accidentally dropped it on Mars Bluff, South Carolina. The core of the bomb was still on the plane, so there wasn't a nuclear explosion, but the 6,000 pounds of conventional high explosives detonated. The bomb fell on a garden in a rural area and created a 35-foot-deep by 75-foot-wide crater and destroyed the nearby house and outbuildings. Fortunately, no one was killed, and there were only minor injuries.

471) The size of the average American new home has almost tripled from 983 square feet in 1950 to 2,600 square feet.

472) Genghis Khan once had a feast with his army while seated on top of Russian army generals and nobility. In 1223 in Russia, the Mongol army had just won the Battle of the Kalka River; the Russian army surrendered, and the Mongols decided to have a celebration feast. The Russian army generals and nobility were forced to lie on the ground, and a heavy wooden gate was thrown on top of them. Chairs and tables were set on top of the gate, and the Mongols sat down for a feast on top of the still living bodies of their enemies.

473) In 1891 when electricity was first installed at the White House, President Benjamin Harrison and his wife were so afraid of being electrocuted that they never touched the light switches; they always had staff turn the lights on and off.

474) Facebook has a blue color scheme because its founder, Mark Zuckerberg, has red-green color blindness, and blue is the color he sees best.

475) During WWI, a Canadian soldier made a black bear his pet and named her Winnipeg. She was known as Winnie when she became a resident of the London Zoological Gardens where a boy named Christopher Robin, son of author A.A. Milne, adored her and named his teddy bear after her.

476) Lemons float in water; limes sink. They both have densities close to that of water, but limes are slightly denser, so they sink.

477) The average Major League Baseball game lasts almost 3 hours, but it only has about 18 minutes of action if you include balls in play, stolen base attempts, pitches, running batters, pickoff throws, etc. If you just include balls in play and runner advancement attempts, there are less than 6 minutes of action.

478) Time passes faster for your face than it does for your feet. The difference is much too small for humans to perceive, but technically, time passes faster at higher elevations because the pull of the Earth's gravitational field is weaker. Researchers have proven the differences even with height differences less than one meter.

479) Pluto hadn't even made one complete revolution around the Sun between its discovery as a planet and its demotion to dwarf planet. Pluto was discovered in 1930, and it takes 248 years for it to complete one rotation around the Sun, so its first birthday (one Pluto year) since discovery won't be until 2178.

480) In 1838, Edgar Allen Poe published the novel *The Narrative of Arthur Gordon Pym of Nantucket* which describes how the crew of a ship called the *Grampus* were adrift in the ocean and drew straws to decide who would be eaten. The losing crew member was Richard Parker who was killed and eaten. Forty-six years later in 1884, a yacht called the *Mignonette* sank, and its four surviving crew escaped in a lifeboat. They eventually decided they were going to have to eat one of their own to survive. They killed and ate a crew member named Richard Parker.

481) Atoms are 99.9999999% empty space. If all the empty space was eliminated, the entire human species would fit into the volume of a sugar cube.

482) In 2009, physicist Stephen Hawking threw a champagne party for time travelers. He didn't put out invitations until after the party hypothesizing that if someone showed up, it would be proof of time travel. No one came.

483) President Martin Van Buren helped to make the word OK popular. One of his nicknames was "Old Kinderhook" based on the town he was from in New York; during his presidential campaign, people held up signs and chanted OK.

484) Chocolate has been used as medicine since at least the 1500s. The Aztecs brewed a drink from cacao and tree bark to treat infections. Children with diarrhea received a drink made from the grounds of cacao beans and other roots. A text from 1552 lists a host of ailments cacao could treat including angina, fatigue, dysentery, gout, hemorrhoids, and even dental problems.

485) Hippos sleep in the water; they surface automatically and breathe without waking up.

486) Female anaconda snakes are on average 4.7 times larger than males; that is the largest size difference between sexes in any land vertebrate.

487) In the Peanuts comic strip, Peppermint Patty's real name is Patricia Reichardt.

488) The world's first human HIV cases occurred sometime between 1884 and 1924 in several sub-Saharan African countries. It wasn't until the 1950s and 1960s that HIV cases first appeared in the Western Hemisphere, and it wouldn't be until the 1980s that HIV and AIDS became a worldwide health concern.

489) Nutmeg can be toxic. In high enough doses, nutmeg can induce hallucinations, convulsions, pain, nausea, and paranoia that can last for several days. It typically takes two teaspoons or more to see toxic symptoms. Nutmeg comes from the seed of a tropical evergreen.

490) Reindeer can see ultraviolet light. The human eye blocks UV light from reaching the retina, and in situations with a lot of reflected UV light like snow, it can damage the eye causing snow blindness. For reindeer who must deal with reflected UV light from arctic snow most of the year, it makes sense they would develop a way of seeing into the

UV light to protect themselves from snow blindness, but it also helps them in their survival. Important things like urine from predators or competitors, fur from predators, and lichen, one of their main food sources in the winter, absorb UV light and appear black against the snow making them easy to see.

491) Shortly after the American Civil War, one-third to one-half of U.S. currency was counterfeit. This was a major threat to the economy, and the Secret Service was founded in 1865 specifically to reduce counterfeit money.

492) Sloths only poop once a week; they also must do it on the ground, making them an easy target for predators. A sloth can lose one-third of its body weight from pooping, and it all comes out in one push. They dig a small hole to go in and cover it up when they are done and head back into the trees.

493) In 1872, P.B.S. Pinchback became the first African American state governor. He had been a Louisiana state senator and was serving as lieutenant governor when Governor Henry Clay Warmoth had to step down temporarily while he battled impeachment charges for election tampering. Pinchback served as governor for 36 days; there wouldn't be another African American governor in the U.S. until 1990.

494) The first pair of corrective eyeglasses was invented in Italy sometime between 1268 and 1300; they were two reading stones (magnifying glasses) connected with a hinge balanced on the bridge of the nose.

495) Cockroaches have existed for about 350 million years; they were around 120 million years before dinosaurs.

496) "Make Your Wet Dreams Come True" was once a U.S. presidential campaign slogan. In 1928, former New York Governor Al Smith ran for president against Herbert Hoover; a major debate was over whether the prohibition alcohol ban should continue. Smith campaigned against prohibition, so they produced buttons bearing the slogan.

497) A mondegreen is a mishearing or misinterpretation of a phrase in a way that gives it a new meaning such as when you mishear the lyrics of a song and insert words that sound similar and make sense.

498) Theodore Roosevelt was the first American to earn a brown belt in judo.

499) Seahorses don't have teeth or stomachs and must eat constantly, so they don't starve.

500) Betty Nesmith, mother of Michael Nesmith of The Monkees pop group, invented Liquid Paper correction fluid in 1956 in her kitchen. She worked as an executive secretary at a bank and began using white tempera paint to cover up typing mistakes. After perfecting the formula, she named it Liquid Paper and began marketing it herself. She eventually sold the rights to the Gillette Corporation in 1979 for $47.5 million plus royalties on future sales.

501) When you blush, your stomach lining also turns red due to increased blood flow throughout the body from the release of adrenaline.

502) Memories continually change. They are malleable and are reconstructed with each recall; what we remember changes each time we recall the event. The slightly changed memory becomes the current memory only to be reconstructed with the next recall.

503) At any given time, there are about 1,800 thunderstorms in progress around the world. About 18 million thunderstorms occur annually worldwide with about 100,000 to 125,000 in the U.S.

504) In 2014 when Queen Elizabeth II visited the *Game of Thrones* set in Belfast, Northern Ireland, she declined an opportunity to sit on the Iron Throne because there is an old tradition that prohibits the reigning English monarch from even sitting on a foreign throne.

505) Giraffes can't cough because their necks are so long that their lungs are too far away from their epiglottis, and coughing is a combination movement of the lungs and epiglottis.

506) FDA regulations allow a certain amount of foreign animal matter to be present in food. For raisins, 10 insects and 35 fruit fly eggs per 8 ounces is acceptable; for peanut butter, 5 rodent hairs and 150 bug fragments in 1 pound is fine.

507) Scientists believe that it rains diamonds on Jupiter and Saturn. Lightning storms turn methane into soot which under pressure hardens into chunks of graphite and then diamond as it falls. The largest diamonds would likely be about a centimeter in diameter and would eventually melt in the hot planet core.

508) The slow loris is the only known venomous primate. They are nocturnal and live in southeast Asia. If they lick a gland under their arms and combine it with their saliva, they have a toxic bite.

509) No one who has walked on the Moon was born after 1935. Charles Duke, the tenth person to walk on the Moon, was born the latest, October 3, 1935.

510) The surface area of your lungs is about the same size as a tennis court.

511) The character of Frasier Crane played by Kelsey Grammer had more consecutive years on U.S. television than any other live action sitcom character; between *Cheers* and *Frasier*, Grammer played Crane for 20 consecutive years.

512) When written out in English, no number before one thousand contains the letter a.

513) Ester Ledecka of the Czech Republic is the first woman to win gold medals in two different sports at the same Winter Olympics. At the 2018 PyeongChang Olympics, she won in skiing and snowboarding.

514) Prior to 1824, no one knew that dinosaurs had existed. Even though the name dinosaur wasn't applied until 1842, William Buckland, a geology professor at Oxford, was the first person to recognize dinosaurs for what they were in 1824 when he used the name Megalosaurus to describe an extinct carnivorous lizard fossil.

515) A photon of light takes about 8 minutes to get from the Sun to the Earth, but it can take a photon 100,000 years to get from the core of the Sun to the surface.

516) The 3 Musketeers candy bar got its name because it originally came in a package with three pieces with different nougat flavors - vanilla, chocolate, and strawberry.

517) Until about 10,000 years ago, all humans had brown eyes. A genetic mutation at about that time produced blue eyes.

518) Niddick is the term for the nape of the neck.

519) Lyme disease gets its name from Lyme, Connecticut, a small coastal town, where several cases were identified in 1975.

520) President John Quincy Adams received a pet alligator as a gift and kept it in the White House East Room bathroom for two months before returning it.

521) Cats have six to eight times more rod cells in their eye compared to humans; the rods are sensitive to low light giving them their superior night vision. Their elliptical eye shape and larger corneas also help gather more light.

522) About 100 cats roam free at Disneyland; they keep the rodent population down and have been in the park since it opened in 1955. They're all spayed, neutered, vaccinated, and tagged and have feeding stations, veterinary care, and are taken care of by the workers.

523) Actress Mariska Hargitay has played the same character on U.S. primetime live action television longer than anyone else male or female. She has played Olivia Benson on *Law & Order: Special Victims Unit* since 1999.

524) Mongolia has the smallest navy in the world with one ship and seven men; it is the world's second largest landlocked country.

525) Tim Berners-Lee, inventor of the World Wide Web, regrets putting the double slashes in URLs; it was a programming convention at the

time, but not necessary and has caused a lot of wasted time typing and wasted paper printing.

526) When Thomas Jefferson sent Lewis and Clark on their expedition, he asked them to look for wooly mammoths; Jefferson believed that there might be wooly mammoths still living in the west.

527) The Sun and Moon appear to be the same size in the sky because the Sun is 400 times larger than the Moon, but it also 400 times further away from the Earth.

528) The device that would evolve into the chainsaw was developed as a childbirth aid. Around 1780, two doctors were trying to create something to help remove bone and cartilage from the birth canal to widen it during problematic childbirths. At the time, this method was preferred to caesarians and was done with a saw and knife. The early chainsaw developed for this purpose looked like a regular knife with a small chain around it which was operated by a hand crank.

529) The first U.S. car race ever was on Thanksgiving Day, November 27, 1895. The *Chicago-Times Herald* sponsored a 54-mile race from downtown Chicago to Evanston and back. The top speed of the winning car was 7 mph.

530) Scientists have tracked Alpine swifts, a swallow-like bird found in Europe, Africa, and Asia, that can fly for 200 days straight, eating and sleeping while flying and never leaving the air.

531) Wisconsin is known as the Badger State because lead miners in the 1830s lived in temporary caves cut into the hillsides which became known as badger dens, and the miners who lived in them were known as badgers.

532) Due to the U.S. Electoral College, you could theoretically win the presidential election with only 23% of the popular vote. This requires winning the required 270 electoral votes in the smallest electoral vote states by one vote in each state and not getting any votes in the largest electoral vote states.

533) Whales, dolphins, orcas and porpoises, have an unusual form of sleep called unihemispheric slow-wave sleep. They shut down only one hemisphere of their brain and close the opposite eye. During this time, the other half of the brain monitors what's happening in their environment and controls breathing functions. Dolphins will sometimes hang motionless at the surface of the water during sleep, or they may swim slowly.

534) The word idiot derives from the ancient Greeks. In ancient Athens, contributing to politics and society was considered the norm and desirable; the overwhelming majority participated in politics in some form. Those who did not contribute were known as "idiotes" which came from the word "idios" meaning the self and were considered apathetic, uneducated, and ignorant.

535) The tradition in the White House Roosevelt Room has been to hang Franklin Delano Roosevelt's portrait over the mantel during Democratic administrations and hang Theodore Roosevelt's equestrian portrait above the mantel during Republican administrations. Whichever painting is not over the mantel is hung on the south wall of the room.

536) South African earthworms are the largest known and can grow as large as 22 feet with the average length being about 6 feet.

537) The word "barbarian" originated in ancient Greece and was used for all non-Greek speaking people. It derives from the Greek word "bárbaros" which meant babbler since the Greeks thought speakers of foreign tongues made unintelligible sounds like "bar bar bar."

538) The sweaters children's television star Mr. Rogers wore on his show were all hand knitted by his mother.

539) Deja reve is the feeling of having already dreamed something that you are now experiencing.

540) The Russian army didn't wear socks until 2013. Since the 17th century, the army had worn portyanki, a square of cloth (cotton for

summer, flannel for winter), which they wrapped their feet in. Portyanki were far cheaper to make than socks, and they were quicker and easier to wash, dry, and mend, but they did have to be worn correctly and wrapped tightly or they could cause blisters. You also had to be able to put your portyanki on fast since regulations required soldiers to be fully dressed in 45 seconds.

541) Gnurr is the word for pocket lint.

542) "Yo Mama" jokes date back to a Babylonian tablet from about 1500 BC; William Shakespeare also told several "Yo Mama" type jokes in his plays.

543) *The Fugitive* in 1967 was the first U.S. television series to feature a final episode where all plot lines were resolved, and all questions were answered.

544) Pocahontas was on the back of the U.S. $20 bill first issued in 1865; the bill went out of circulation in the late 1800s.

545) Slave-maker ants will take over the nest of other ants, and when the new ants hatch, they become slaves of the colony.

546) Along with being a world-famous escape artist, Harry Houdini was an aviation pioneer; he made the first controlled powered flight of an airplane in Australia in 1910.

547) Humans make up about 0.01% of the Earth's biomass; plants account for about 80%; bacteria account for 13%, and fungus are 2%. Animals as a whole account for about 0.36% with insects making up about half of that and fish accounting for another third.

548) Queen Elizabeth II doesn't have a passport because passports are issued in her name and on her authority, so it would be superfluous for her to have one.

549) To avoid capture, Nedeljko Čabrinović, one of the men involved in the assassination of Archduke Franz Ferdinand in Sarajevo in 1914, swallowed a cyanide capsule and jumped into the River Miljacka to kill

himself. Unfortunately, the cyanide pill had expired and failed to kill him, and the River Miljacka was only about four inches deep. He was captured by police, and since he was still a minor, he was sentenced to 20 years in prison instead of execution; he died in prison of tuberculosis.

550) A spider's muscles pull its legs inward, but they can't push them out again. To push them out, it must pump a watery liquid into its legs.

551) Pregnancy tests have existed for about 3,400 years. Ancient Egyptian women urinated on a bag of barley and a bag of wheat; if the grain in either bag sprouted, she was pregnant. If the barley sprouted first, it would be a boy; if the wheat sprouted first, it would be a girl. A test done in 1963 found that the method was accurate about 70% of the time in determining pregnancy but wasn't accurate in determining the baby's gender.

552) The night Abraham Lincoln was assassinated he had a bodyguard, but he had left his post to have a drink at the Star Saloon next to Ford's Theatre. John Frederick Parker was the police officer assigned to guard Lincoln and was initially seated outside the president's box. To be able to see the play, he moved to the first gallery, and at intermission, he joined the footman and coachman for Lincoln's carriage for drinks next door. It isn't clear if he returned to the theater at all, but he wasn't at his post outside Lincoln's box when John Wilkes Booth shot him. Ironically, Booth had been at the same saloon working up his courage. In November 1864, the Washington police force created the first permanent detail to protect the president; it was made up of four officers. Parker had a spotty record but was somehow named to the detail and drew the assignment for that night. The Secret Service did not begin protecting the president until 1901 after the assassination of President William McKinley.

553) Tsundoku is the act of acquiring books and not reading them.

554) Based on his medical records which were auctioned off in 2012, Adolf Hitler had a huge problem with flatulence. He was regularly taking 28 different drugs to try to control it. Some of the anti-gas pills

he used contained a base of strychnine which caused further stomach and liver issues.

555) A Munchausen number, also known as a perfect digit-to-digit invariant, is a natural number that is equal to the sum of its digits each raised to the power of itself. For example, 3435 is a Munchausen number because $3435 = 3^3 + 4^4 + 3^3 + 5^5$. In base 10 numbers, there are only four Munchausen numbers: 0, 1, 3435, and 438579088.

556) Cleopatra spoke as many as a dozen languages and was educated in mathematics, philosophy, oratory, and astronomy. She is often portrayed as being an incomparable beauty and little else, but there is also evidence that she wasn't as physically striking as once believed.

557) Frogs can't swallow with their eyes open. Since they don't have muscles to chew their food, they use their eyes to force their food down their throats. Their eyes sink down inside their skull to push the food down.

558) Male goats urinate on their own heads to smell more attractive to females.

559) Some people who get bitten by the lone star tick can develop a sudden allergy to red meat. The allergy affects the sensitivity to a carbohydrate called galactose-alpha-1,3-galactose which is in most mammal cell membranes, so the allergy doesn't extend to poultry or seafood. The lone star tick has been recorded as far north as Maine and as far west as central Texas and Oklahoma.

560) In languages all over the world, there are more names for warm colors (red, orange, yellow) than there are for cool colors (green, blue, purple).

561) As part of its reproductive process, the jewel wasp will sting a cockroach twice, first in the thorax to partially immobilize it and then in the head to block its normal escape reflex. The wasp is too small to carry the cockroach, so it leads it back to its burrow by pulling on one of its antennae. Once in the burrow, the wasp lays one egg on the

roach's abdomen and exits and fills in the burrow entrance with pebbles. With the effect of the wasp venom, the roach rests in the burrow, and in about three days, the wasp's egg hatches, and the larva begins feeding on the roach for four to five days before chewing its way into the roach's abdomen. It continues to reside inside the roach, and over a period of eight days, it consumes the roach's internal organs in an order that maximizes the time the roach is still alive. The larva enters a pupal stage and forms a cocoon inside the roach, and the fully-grown wasp eventually emerges from the roach's body completing the reproductive cycle.

562) While there are more than 60 species of eagles worldwide, only two species, the bald eagle and the golden eagle, live in North America.

563) The skin on a whale shark's back can be up to four inches thick, and they can make it even tougher by clenching the muscles just beneath the skin. Their underbellies are relatively soft and vulnerable, so they will often turn their belly away when approached.

564) Opossums don't play dead; if frightened, they go into shock which induces a comatose state that can last from 40 minutes to 4 hours.

565) The words bulb, angel, and month have no rhyming words in the English language.

566) Kinderschema is a set of physical characteristics that humans are naturally drawn towards; the characteristics include a rounded belly, big head, big eyes, loose limbs, etc. Puppies, kittens, and other animals including human babies trigger kinderschema. Humans have an intrinsic motivation to care for babies and children; these tendencies have developed through millions of years of evolution.

567) One regular 12 ounce can of Coca-Cola contains 10 teaspoons of sugar which is about the recommended amount of sugar for an adult for an entire day.

568) Drupelets are the individual bumps making up a raspberry or blackberry

569) Typewriter is the longest English word that can be made using the letters on only one row of the keyboard.

570) Worf, played by Michael Dorn, is the only *Star Trek* character to appear regularly on two different *Star Trek* series; he appeared on both *Star Trek: The Next Generation* and *Star Trek: Deep Space Nine*.

571) Hitler, Stalin, and Mussolini were all nominated for the Nobel Peace Prize.

572) The difference in time between the Stegosaurus and Tyrannosaurus Rex is larger than the time between the Tyrannosaurus and you. Stegosaurus existed about 150 million years ago; Tyrannosaurus Rex didn't evolve until about 67 million years ago, so the two were separated by about 83 million years.

573) Australia has over 860 different reptile species, more than any other country in the world. They include lizards, crocodiles, turtles, and snakes. North America only has 280 reptile species.

574) The human eye has enough visual acuity that you could see a candle flame 30 miles away on a dark night if the Earth was flat.

575) For the television series *M\*A\*S\*H*, Alan Alda was the first person to win acting, writing, and directing Emmys for the same series.

576) In the Middle Ages, men who wanted a boy sometimes had their left testicle removed because people believed that the right testicle made boy sperm, and the left made girl sperm.

577) The first movie ever to release a soundtrack recording was *Snow White and the Seven Dwarfs* in 1938.

578) Only 45% of the London Underground is underground.

579) Benito Mussolini wrote a historical romance novel called *The Cardinal's Mistress*.

580) Like many royal houses, the Ptolemaic dynasty of Cleopatra often married within the family to preserve bloodline purity. More than a

dozen of Cleopatra's ancestors wed cousins or siblings, and it's likely that her parents were brother and sister.

581) Due to continental drift, New York City moves one inch further away from London each year.

582) A Japanese men's marathon runner at the 1912 Stockholm Olympics ended up with an official finishing time of 54 years, 8 months, 6 days, 5 hours, 32 minutes and 20.3 seconds. Shizo Kanakuri was an experienced runner and held the 25-mile world record when he went to the Stockholm games; he started the race, but temperatures of almost 90 degrees Fahrenheit forced him to drop out after more than 18 miles. He did not notify the officials, and feeling ashamed that he did not finish, he went quietly back to Japan and was listed as missing in the results. In 1967, a Swedish television show started looking for the missing marathon runner, and at the age of 75, Kanakuri was invited to Sweden for the 55th anniversary of the 1912 games where he was given the opportunity to finish the race and receive an official time.

583) Kentucky produces about 95% of the bourbon in the world and has an inventory of 7.5 million barrels, almost two barrels for each of its 4.3 million residents.

584) Based on volume, all the humans in the world could fit in a cube 2,577 feet on each side or about 0.116 cubic miles.

585) The saltwater crocodile is the world's largest reptile. They are up to 20 feet long and 3,000 pounds.

586) Due to erosion, Niagara Falls has receded about seven miles over the last 12,500 years.

587) The Walt Disney Company is the largest consumer of fireworks in the world and the second largest purchaser of explosive devices behind the U.S. Department of Defense.

588) The Spanish national anthem "Marcha Real" has no words; it is one of four national anthems in the world along with Bosnia and Herzegovina, Kosovo, and San Marino that have no official lyrics.

589) A semordnilap is a word that makes a completely different word spelled backwards, for example stressed and desserts. The word semordnilap is palindromes spelled backwards.

590) The tall, pleated chef's hat is called a toque; the 100 folds in the toque are said to represent 100 ways to cook an egg.

591) There are so many possible iterations of a game of chess that no one has been able to calculate it accurately. In the 1950s, mathematician Claude Shannon came up with what is now known as the Shannon Number to estimate the possible iterations at between $10^{111}$ and $10^{123}$. In comparison, there are $10^{81}$ atoms in the known universe.

592) King Louis XIV who ruled France from 1643-1715 was offered plans for the first bacteriological weapon by an Italian chemist; he refused instantly and paid the scientist to keep the deadly discovery a secret.

593) Pringles aren't a potato chip because they are made from dehydrated potato flakes pressed together rather than thinly sliced potatoes, so they can't be marketed as a chip but instead are a crisp.

594) American microbiologist Maurice Ralph Hilleman (1919-2005) is credited with saving more lives than any other medical scientist of the 20th century. He specialized in developing vaccines and developed over 40 in his career including 8 of the 14 vaccines routinely recommended: measles, mumps, hepatitis A, hepatitis B, chickenpox, meningitis, pneumonia, and Haemophilus influenzae.

595) If you don't swing your arms while walking, it requires about 12% more effort to walk which is equivalent to walking about 20% faster.

596) Hawaiian pizza is Canadian; it was invented in 1962 in Ontario, Canada.

597) The American television series *Royal Pains* (2009-2016) featured the second largest private home ever built in the United States. The mansion that the character Boris Kuester von Jurgens-Ratenicz lived in is the 109,000 square foot Oheka Castle in West Hills, New York which was built from 1914-1919 for Otto Hermann Kahn.

598) The nursery rhyme *Mary Had a Little Lamb* is based on the true story of Mary Sawyer of Sterling, Massachusetts who as an 11-year-old was followed to school by her pet lamb. John Roulstone, a student a year or two older, handed Mary a piece of paper the next day with a poem he had written about it. In 1830, Sarah Josepha Hale, a well-known writer and editor, published *Poems for Our Children* which included a version of the poem.

599) Wells Fargo has an ATM in McMurdo Station, Antarctica. A maintenance person only shows up to service it every two years.

600) A pair of brown rats can produce 2,000 descendants in a year and up to 500 million descendants in three years.

# Facts 601-900

601) About 12% of people dream entirely in black and white. The exposure to color television seems to have had a significant impact on whether people dream in color; people who grew up with little access to color television dream in black and white about 25% of the time. In the 1940s before color television, the numbers were reversed with about 75% of people reporting they dreamed in black and white.

602) In 1959, the U.S. Navy submarine USS Barbero assisted the U.S. Post Office Department in a test to deliver mail via a cruise missile. The submarine launched a cruise missile with 3,000 pieces of mail from Norfolk, Virginia, and it landed at its target in Mayport, Florida 22 minutes later. While the success of the test was lauded at the time, it never went any further since the cost could not be justified.

603) On a clear night in a dark area, you can see about 2,000 stars in the sky.

604) The first pedestrian ever killed by a car occurred on August 17, 1896. Bridget Driscoll was struck by a demonstration car which was traveling at 4 mph.

605) Huh is the closest thing to a universal word. It means the same thing in every language, and everybody in almost every language says it.

606) Of the 10 largest private homes ever built in the U.S., nine were built in 1932 or earlier; and four were built in the 1880s and 1890s.

607) The magma chamber of hot and partly molten rock beneath Yellowstone National Park is large enough to fill the 1,000 cubic mile Grand Canyon 11 times over.

608) A series of earthquakes in 1811 and 1812 originating in Missouri raised the soil beneath the Mississippi River and temporarily changed its course so that it flowed backward.

609) Richard Anderson and Martin E. Brooks were the first actors in U.S. television history to play the same characters on two different series on two different networks at the same time. They played Oscar Goldman and Dr. Rudy Wells on *The Six Million Dollar Man* and *The Bionic Woman*; both shows were originally on ABC before *The Bionic Woman* moved to NBC in 1978 for its last season, and they continued their roles on both shows.

610) Charlie Chaplin didn't release his first film with sound until 13 years after the first talkie.

611) Roman charioteer Gaius Appuleius Diocles who lived in the 2nd century was one of the most celebrated ancient athletes and may be the best paid athlete of all time. He raced four horse chariots, and records show he won 1,462 out of the 4,257 races he competed in. He also seemed to be a showman making many of his victories come from behind last second victories which made him even more popular. He raced for 24 years and retired at age 42. His winnings amounted to the equivalent of 2,600 kg of gold which considering the buying power at the time would make him a multi-billionaire in today's dollars.

612) By area, 38% of the United States is further north than the most southern point of Canada. Middle Island in Lake Erie at 41.7 degrees north latitude is the southernmost point of land in Canada and is about the same latitude as Chicago.

613) *Fantasia* in 1940 has the first appearance of Mickey Mouse in a Disney animated feature.

614) A dog's shoulder blades are somewhat unattached to the rest of the skeleton to allow greater flexibility for running. They have what is also referred to as floating shoulders which aren't attached to any bones at the top but do have several muscle and ligament attachments.

615) Originally, the term third world country did not mean a developing country. It was coined during the Cold War in 1952 by a French demographer and referred simply to countries that weren't aligned with either the U.S. or Soviet Union.

616) The last guillotining in France occurred on September 10, 1977.

617) Caterpillars have up to 4,000 muscles including 248 muscles in their head alone; humans have about 650 muscles total.

618) President Thomas Jefferson wasn't fond of formal events, and he often greeted foreign dignitaries in his pajamas.

619) The first phone book consisting of a single piece of cardboard was published February 21, 1878 in New Haven, Connecticut; it had 50 listings.

620) The letter x likely became the symbol for a kiss because in the Middle Ages most people were illiterate and would sign documents with an x and then kiss it to show their sincerity.

621) Although official records don't exist for safety reasons, 7'4" actor and wrestler Andre the Giant, who weighed over 500 pounds and had an incredible tolerance for alcohol, drank 156 beers in a single sitting. That is over 14.5 gallons.

622) When mating, flatworms compete to see which one can inject sperm into the other; the winner becomes the father; the loser becomes the mother. Flatworms are hermaphroditic having both male and female reproductive organs.

623) Wombats are the only animal in the world with cube shaped poop. It appears to be due to the irregular shape and elasticity of their intestines.

624) Barnacle geese chicks must jump off cliffs sometimes hundreds of feet high when they are at little as one day old and can't fly. Barnacle geese, which nest in the Arctic, protect their young from predators by nesting on high ledges and cliffs. They can't feed the babies in the nest, and the chicks must eat within 36 hours, so to get to the grass they need to eat, they must jump from their nest and hope to survive. Fortunately, the chicks are light and fluffy and usually survive the fall even after bouncing off rocks.

625) A group of Purdue engineering students made a licking machine modeled after a human tongue and found that it took an average of 364 licks to get to the center of a Tootsie Pop.

626) A college football game registered as an earthquake. The Earthquake Game was played between LSU and Auburn on October 8, 1988 at LSU's Tiger Stadium before a crowd of 79,431 spectators. Auburn led 6-0 with less than two minutes left when LSU drove down the field and eventually threw an 11-yard touchdown pass on fourth down. The crowd's reaction to the touchdown pass registered as an earthquake on a seismograph located about 1,000 feet from the stadium at LSU's Howe-Russell Geoscience Complex. A seismologist noticed the reading the next day.

627) We don't know how many insect species exist; new beetles are discovered at a rate of one an hour. There are 350,000 named beetles, plus perhaps 8 million more unnamed.

628) There is enough water in Lake Superior to cover all the land in North and South America in one foot of water.

629) At up to 7 feet tall and 1,500 pounds, the moose is the largest species of deer.

630) Grawlix is a string of typographical symbols (e.g. %@$&*!) used in place of an obscenity.

631) In Colombia and other South American countries, movie theaters sell spicy roasted ants that are munched the way American's enjoy popcorn.

632) Even though it is almost 300 miles from the ocean, Reno, Nevada is about 86 miles further west than Los Angeles.

633) At its peak in the 1990s when it was mailing out CDs to get people to sign up for internet service, AOL was producing 50% of all CDs being made in the world.

634) Uncoiled, a Slinky is 87 feet long.

635) The whale shark is the largest current day shark; they can be up to 41 feet long and 47,000 pounds.

636) When he first appeared in 1938, the original comics Superman couldn't fly; he could only jump the very specific distance of one-eighth of a mile. His flying ability first appeared in cartoons and radio plays; it wouldn't appear in comics until 1941.

637) A domestic cat can run up to 30 mph in a short spurt; the fastest speed a human has ever run is about 28 mph.

638) The standard U.S. railroad width of 4 feet 8.5 inches is directly derived from the width of Roman war chariots. The English expatriates who designed the U.S. railroad system based their measurements on the pre-railroad tramways built in England. Those tramways were built using the same tools used to build wagons which were also that width. Wagons were built to fit the ruts carved out by Roman war chariots; otherwise, they would break during long treks across the old English roads which were built by the Romans. All Roman chariots were built to a standard width of 4 feet 8.5 inches.

639) Almost 3% of the ice in the Antarctic glaciers is from penguin urine.

640) There is a secret basketball court for staff tucked inside the empty upper third of the mountain that makes up the Matterhorn ride at Disneyland.

641) When dissolved in water, small concentrations of Viagra can double the shelf life of cut flowers, making them stand up straight for as long as a week beyond their natural lifespan.

642) The little paper tail sticking out of a Hershey's Kiss is called a niggly wiggly.

643) *I Love Lucy* in 1951 was the first U.S. television show to end while it was still at the top of the Nielsen Ratings.

644) Giant anteaters eat up to 30,000 ants a day while still sleeping 16 hours a day.

645) A baby owl is called an owlet.

646) Killing or attempting to kill a U.S. president wasn't a federal offense until 1965, two years after John F. Kennedy's death.

647) Cats and humans have almost identical brain structures including the region which controls emotion. Cats have temporal, occipital, frontal and parietal lobes in their brains just like humans, and their brains also contain gray and white matter like humans, and the connections within their brains seem to mirror those of humans. Their brains release neurotransmitters like humans, and they have short and long-term memory.

648) Joseph Stalin plotted to kill John Wayne and sent two men to pose as FBI agents to assassinate him. Stalin was a big film fan and considered Wayne a threat to the Soviet Union because of his strong anti-communist beliefs.

649) Contrary to what we see today, ancient Greek sculptures were painted in bold primary colors. Between the use of special ultraviolet lamps and passages in Greek literature that refer to colored statues, it's clear that statues were originally colored, and they only look the way they do today because the color has worn off.

650) Humans domesticated the horse around 4500 BC; the saddle was invented as early as 800 BC, but the stirrup probably wasn't created until about 300 BC.

651) Albert Einstein co-invented a refrigerator. The coolants used in the original refrigerators were toxic and could leak; Einstein got involved when he read about a Berlin family killed in their sleep by leaking coolant. In 1926, he worked with one of his former students, Leo Szilardtor, to develop a refrigerator with no moving parts, so there were no seals to potentially leak. It operated at constant pressure and

only required a heat source to operate and was patented in the U.S. in 1930.

652) A zarf is the piece of cardboard that goes around your hot cup of coffee.

653) The Onagadori chicken of Japan has the world's longest feathers; its tail feathers can measure over 10 meters.

654) In humans, the right lung is always larger than the left. The left lung is smaller to leave enough room for the heart.

655) In 1879, Liege, Belgium attempted to use 37 cats as mail carriers. Messages were placed in waterproof bags the cats carried around their necks. Not surprisingly, the cats proved to be unreliable and slow, taking many hours or a day to deliver the mail, and the service didn't last long.

656) In ancient Egypt, if a patient died during surgery, the surgeon's hands were cut off.

657) In 1946, Nutella was invented by an Italian pastry maker who was looking for a cheaper alternative to chocolate which was in short supply due to WWII, so he mixed hazelnuts with some cocoa.

658) The oldest surviving photograph in existence was taken in 1826 by French photography pioneer Joseph Nicéphore Niépce. It is the view from the window of an estate in Burgundy, France and was taken with an eight-hour exposure and was made on a pewter plate using asphalt.

659) From the 1830s to the 1930s, the collars on men's dress shirts were typically detachable; this was to save on laundry since the collar is the part that most frequently needs cleaning.

660) Without a visual reference point, humans are incapable of walking in a straight line. If blindfolded or lost in terrain devoid of landmarks, we tend to walk in circles. Scientists have yet been unable to determine why.

661) Between 1935 and 1945, the secret German government program Lebensborn encouraged suitable women to bear children to create racially pure Aryans for the Third Reich. Women in the program were required to hand their children over to the SS to be raised. The program originally started in Germany but spread to other occupied European countries during WWII. Estimates are that there were about 20,000 Lebensborn children born; the most famous is ABBA singer Anni-Frid Lyngstad who was born of a Norwegian mother and a German sergeant.

662) Due to a global surge in jellyfish populations, nuclear power plants around the world are experiencing an increasing number of outages caused by jellyfish clogging cooling water intakes. Outages have occurred in Japan, Israel, Scotland, and the United States. The surging populations are likely due to overfishing reducing predation and the jellyfish's ability to withstand increasing ocean acidity levels.

663) The pope can't be an organ donor. According to the Vatican, his body belongs to the Catholic Church and must be buried intact.

664) On average, it takes about a minute for human blood to circulate through the entire body.

665) The largest cell in the human body is the egg which is about 30 times larger than the smallest cell, sperm.

666) Ronald Wayne was the third co-founder and a 10% shareholder of Apple Computer; in 1976, he sold his stake for $800.

667) During WWI, starving wolves displaced by the war amassed in such numbers that the Germans and Russians agreed to a temporary cease fire to jointly battle the wolves.

668) In the 1920s when insulin was still harvested from animals, it took 10,000 pounds of pig pancreases to make 1 pound of concentrated insulin.

669) Arachibutyrophobia is the fear of peanut butter sticking to the roof of your mouth.

670) About 85% of humans only breathe out of one nostril at a time. They switch between nostrils about every four hours although it varies by person, body position, and other factors.

671) The Macy's Thanksgiving Day Parade used to intentionally release the giant inflatable balloon characters into the sky after the parade. The very first balloons would pop quickly, but in 1929, they added safety valves so the helium would slowly leak out allowing the balloons to float for days. They also tagged the balloons with return addresses, so they could be sent back to Macy's which would reward the finders with gifts. They quit releasing the balloons after the 1932 parade when a balloon wrapped around an airplane's wing sending it into a tailspin; luckily, there were no fatalities.

672) The first mutiny in space occurred on *Skylab 4* on December 28th, 1973. The three-man crew turned off radio communications with NASA for a full day and spent the day relaxing. They had already spent about as much time in space as anyone ever had and were tired of the demanding schedule NASA had set for them. After the day off, they continued their duties and spent about another month in space setting the record at the time of 84 days.

673) Foreign accent syndrome is extremely rare and typically caused by stroke or brain injury and affects the way a person forms words giving the perception they are speaking with a foreign accent.

674) While a queen ant can live for up to 30 years, male ants typically only live for a few weeks, and workers live for several months.

675) The expression "caught red-handed" originated as a reference to someone killing or poaching an animal that didn't belong to them and being caught with the blood on their hands.

676) Adult dogs have 42 teeth; puppies have 28 baby teeth.

677) Tear gas has been banned in warfare since 1993, but it is still used in domestic law enforcement.

678) The placebo effect works even if people know it is a placebo. In studies, if people were told the pill they were taking was a placebo but were also told that placebos can have an effect, they experienced the same outcome as those unknowingly taking a placebo.

679) Ice worms are related to common earthworms but spend their entire lives in glaciers and require below freezing temperatures to survive. They are found across the northern United States and Canada in Alaska, Washington, Oregon and British Columbia and come to the surface of the glaciers to feed on snow algae. At temperatures even five degrees above freezing, their internal membranes start to fall apart, and they essentially liquefy and die.

680) A butt is an actual measurement unit for wine; a buttload of wine is 126 U.S. gallons.

681) Traffic roundabouts have 16 points of conflict where there are chances to hit a pedestrian or another car; comparatively, a four-way intersection has 56. That is why roundabouts are safer than regular intersections, and they also speed up travel by avoiding a lot of stopping.

682) In medieval times, a moment was a unit of time equal to 1/40th of an hour. An hour was defined as 1/12th of the time between sunrise and sunset, so the length of an hour depended on the time of year. Therefore, the length of a moment wasn't fixed either, but on average, it corresponded to 90 seconds.

683) Thomas Jefferson kept a pair of grizzly bear cubs in a cage on the front lawn of the White House for a few months. They were a gift, and he decided they were too dangerous to keep and bequeathed them to a museum.

684) Humans produce about 1.5 quarts of mucus per day and swallow most of it.

685) Squirrels cause about 10-20% of all power outages in the United States. Squirrel outages tend to be more localized and more quickly fixed than those caused by storms.

686) To produce one pound of honey, a hive of bees must visit 2 million flowers and fly about 55,000 miles. One bee colony can produce 60 to 100 pounds of honey per year. An average worker bee makes only about 1/12 of a teaspoon of honey in its lifetime and has a lifespan of about two months; queen bees typically live for three to five years.

687) There is a chunk of Africa stuck under the United States. When the supercontinent Pangaea broke apart about 250 million years ago, a chunk of Africa was left behind; it is located near Alabama, just off the coast.

688) Snails move at a steady pace with a maximum speed of about 50 yards per hour or 0.03 mph.

689) Jupiter's red spot, which is a storm, has been shrinking for 150 years; it was once large enough to fit more than three Earths. The spot is growing taller as it gets smaller.

690) The Trans-Siberian Railway in Russia has 3,901 bridges along its 5,772 miles.

691) September is the most popular birth month in the U.S.; the time between September 9 and September 20 contains a majority of the 10 most popular birthdates. September is popular due to holiday conceptions nine months earlier.

692) Without its mucus lining, your stomach would digest itself. Stomach ulcers are areas where the stomach begins to digest itself.

693) Ancient Rome had a four-story shopping mall called Trajan's Market with 150 shops and offices. It was built around 110 AD, and its ruins can still be visited today.

694) The longest English words with no repeating letters are two 15-letter words: uncopyrightable and dermatoglyphics, the study of skin markings.

695) When poured, hot water has a higher pitch than cold water. Water changes viscosity with temperature which affects the sound when poured.

696) Mordhau is a German swordsmanship technique where you hold the sword inverted with both hands gripping the blade and hit the opponent with the pommel or crossguard. The sword acts as a mace or hammer; the technique was mainly used in armored combat.

697) Most members of the nightshade family – tomatoes, potatoes, eggplants, green peppers – contain small quantities of nicotine.

698) Ancient Egyptians were very tolerant of genetic and medical disorders. For example, dwarfism was quite common, and dwarfs were highly respected. Pharaoh Amenemope wrote that caring for the old, the sick, and the malformed was a moral duty.

699) Male giraffes determine whether a female is fertile and ready to mate by tasting her urine. The male bumps the female until she urinates and then tastes the urine for hormones indicating she is in heat.

700) The vinculum is the line between two numbers in a fraction.

701) The king rat can go longer without drinking than any other land animal; they can go their entire life of three to five years without drinking.

702) Quincunx is an arrangement of five objects with four at the corners of a square or rectangle and the fifth at its center such as the number five on dice.

703) The television series *South Park* has a Guinness World Record for the most swearing in an animated television series.

704) Fifty years after it was sent and thirteen years after Western Union shut down its telegram business, Robert Fink received the last Western Union telegram ever delivered in 2019. The telegram congratulated him on his college graduation in 1969 and had been lost in old filing cabinets until someone discovered it and tracked him down to deliver it.

705) The surface area of Pluto is only about 3% larger than Russia.

706) Parts of Canada have less gravity than they should. Since gravity is a result of mass, varying densities of the Earth at different locations can affect it. However, the Hudson Bay region of Canada has a larger variation; the average resident weighs about a tenth of an ounce less than they would weigh elsewhere. The explanation appears to be the melting of the two-mile-thick Laurentide Ice Sheet which started melting about 21,000 years ago and is almost gone. The ice sheet left an indent in the Earth which means less mass and less gravity.

707) Actor Bill Murray has no agent or manager, and anyone wanting to work with him must call a 1-800 number. There is no recorded voicemail message; there is only a menu where you record and send the message. He does have a cell phone for family and friends, but he doesn't use it for business.

708) On January 23, 1916, Browning, Montana experienced the greatest temperature variation ever recorded in a 24-hour period going from a high of 44 degrees to a low of -56 degrees Fahrenheit for a 100-degree change.

709) Patty Duke is the youngest person to have a self-titled U.S. television show. She was 16 years old when *The Patty Duke Show* debuted in 1963.

710) Owyhee is the original English spelling of Hawaii.

711) About 25% of people in the U.S. with two-car garages don't have room to park cars inside them.

712) The Maine state flower isn't a flower; it is the white pinecone and tassel.

713) In 1977, newly inaugurated President Jimmy Carter pardoned draft dodgers, but only about half came back to the U.S.

714) About 1 in every 200 people is born with an extra rib called a cervical rib which forms above the first rib at the base of the neck just above the collarbone. You can have a cervical rib on either or both sides, and it can be a fully formed bony rib or a thin strand of tissue fibers.

715) When a flea jumps, its acceleration is so intense that they must withstand 100 times the force of gravity. Humans pass out at about 5 times the force of gravity.

716) Human embryos develop fingerprints three months after conception.

717) Between 1853 and 1859, New York spent $7.4 million buying the 843 acres for Central Park; comparatively, the United States spent $7.2 million in 1867 to buy Alaska which is 663,268 square miles or 424 million acres.

718) There is enough stone in the Great Pyramid of Giza to build a two-foot-tall by four-inch-wide wall around the entire Earth.

719) According to research, zebras likely evolved to have stripes to avoid biting flies. In an experiment, horses wearing a striped pattern coat had far fewer flies land on the them than horses wearing a solid color coat. The flies spent the same amount of time circling regardless of color, but far fewer landed with stripes.

720) Less than 1% of bacteria cause disease in humans.

721) The human body is bioluminescent; it is just too faint for our eyes to see. A 2009 study found that human bioluminescence in visible light exists; the human body glimmers, but the intensity of the light emitted is 1,000 times lower than the sensitivity of our eyes.

722) On average, a person will die from complete lack of sleep faster than from starvation. You can live about 11 days without sleep but weeks without food.

723) According to the CDC, studies have shown that 50% of American adults will develop at least one mental illness in their lifetime.

724) In 1859 in what was labeled the Pig War, the United States and Great Britain nearly went to war over a pig. A few years earlier, the Oregon Treaty had been signed ending a border dispute between the U.S. and Britain. Citizens of both countries lived on San Juan Island off the coast of what is now Washington state, and a pig belonging to the British wandered onto the land of an American farmer and was shot and killed. Tensions spread into the rest of the community, and the governor of British Columbia sent three warships to the area. The two sides continued to escalate over the following month until British Navy Admiral Robert L. Baynes arrived and ended things by saying that he would not go to war over a pig.

725) Since 1980, the birthrate for human twins has increased about 75%. Part of the reason is that older mothers are more likely to have twins.

726) The average person has four to six dreams per night.

727) Three-digit emergency phone numbers were first introduced in London in 1937 after a fire killed five people, and the person calling for the fire brigade was kept waiting by the operator. The original number was 999.

728) With nine wins, the movie *Butch Cassidy and the Sundance Kid* holds the British Academy Awards (BAFTAs) record.

729) The baobab tree can store up to 32,000 gallons of water in its trunk. Various species are native to Africa, Australia, and India; it can grow to almost 100 feet tall with a trunk diameter up to 36 feet and can live for thousands of years. Because it stores such large volumes of

water in its trunk, elephants, eland, and other animals chew the bark during dry seasons.

730) A double rainbow happens when light is reflected twice in the raindrop. You see two different reflections coming from different angles, and it also reverses the order of the colors on the secondary rainbow.

731) Sandy Island was an island about the size of Manhattan off the coast of Australia that was supposedly discovered by Captain James Cook in 1876 and appeared on maps from 1908 until 2012 when it was discovered that it didn't exist. There is speculation that Cook may have seen a raft of floating pumice ejected by underwater volcanos and mistaken it for an island, but no one is sure.

732) Playboy founder Hugh Hefner is buried next to Marilyn Monroe in a crypt in Los Angeles' Westwood Village Memorial Park cemetery.

733) Penguins can swim as fast as they can because they have a "bubble boost" where they fluff their feathers and release bubbles that reduce the density of the water around them. The bubbles act as lubrication that decreases water viscosity.

734) Human boogers are just dried mucus. Most mucus is swept by the nose cilia hair to the back of the throat, but some near your nostrils can begin to dry out first and become too thick to be swept by the cilia. If it sits long enough, it dries further and becomes a booger.

735) Men account for about 90% of all shark attacks in the world. The reason is behavioral with men more frequently participating in the activities that put you at greatest risk for shark attack such as surfing, diving, and long-distance swimming. As women participate more in some of these risker activities, the number of female attacks is on the rise.

736) Despite its western fame, the Pony Express was only in operation for 18 months from April 1860 to October 1861. The route ran from St.

Joseph, Missouri to Sacramento, California and could transport a letter over 1,800 miles in 10 days.

737) Since 1869, over a million people have been buried on Hart Island which has served as the burial place for New York City's unclaimed bodies. The island is at the western end of Long Island Sound and is one mile long by one-third mile wide.

738) Most artificial banana flavoring is based on an older variety of banana that is no longer grown in bulk, so it doesn't taste very similar to the bananas you buy and eat. The bananas you eat today are mostly the Cavendish variety, but banana flavoring is based on the Gros Michel, a sweeter variety. The Gros Michel is no longer grown in bulk because it is susceptible to a fungus.

739) In 1999 in North Carolina, a female skydiver's life was saved when her chutes didn't open, and she landed on a mound of fire ants. She was jumping from 14,500 feet when her main parachute didn't open; her backup chute opened at 700 feet and quickly deflated. She hit the ground at about 80 mph landing on a mound of fire ants which bit her over 200 times. Fire ants have a toxin filled painful bite which can cause death in some cases. In this case, doctors determined that the repeated fire ant stings shocked her heart and stimulated her nerves and kept her heart beating and her organs functioning long enough to keep her alive during transport. She suffered shattered bones and was in a coma for two weeks, but she recovered fully.

740) Jamais vu is the opposite of déjà vu; it's the feeling you get when you experience something you are already very familiar with, but it feels completely new to you, like it is your first time.

741) If the original Barbie doll was a real woman, she would be 5'9" tall and weigh 110 pounds with measurements of 39-18-33 and wear a size 3 shoe. She would have a body mass index of 16.2 which would make her anorexic, and she wouldn't be able to menstruate.

742) Wooly mammoths were still alive about 900 years after the Great Pyramid of Giza was built. The last mammoths died out about 1650 BC

on Wrangel Island in the Arctic Ocean; the Great Pyramid was completed in about 2560 BC.

743) Excluding eye injuries, pirates likely wore eye patches to see in the dark. They were constantly going above and below deck, and it takes the human eye up to 25 minutes to adapt to seeing in the dark. By wearing a patch, they kept one eye dark adjusted, so they could see in the dark immediately by just moving the eye patch whether for normal duties or for fighting.

744) Manatees control their buoyancy by farting. They can regulate the distribution of their intestinal gases, holding it in when they want to approach the surface and letting loose when it's time to sink.

745) The only WWII U.S. mainland combat deaths occurred on May 5, 1945 when a Japanese balloon bomb exploded and killed a woman and five children in Oregon. The balloon bombs had a 33-foot diameter balloon with 35 pounds of explosives and were designed to rise to 30,000 feet and ride the jet stream east, making it from Japan to the U.S. in about three days. An altimeter would trigger a reaction that would jettison the bombs. Japan released about 9,000 of the bombs. A Sunday school teacher and five students happened upon an unexploded balloon bomb on the ground; it exploded while they were investigating it.

746) Of the first five U.S. presidents, three died on July 4th. John Adams and Thomas Jefferson both died on July 4, 1826; James Monroe, died five years later on July 4, 1831.

747) When you wake up with a jolt, it is called a hypnic jerk. It is an involuntary twitch that occurs when you are beginning to fall asleep causing you to jump and awaken suddenly for a moment.

748) The largest currency denomination ever printed in the U.S. is the 1934 $100,000 bill which featured a picture of Woodrow Wilson. It was only printed for three weeks in December 1934 and January 1935, and they were only used for official transactions between Federal Reserve Banks.

749) If you've ever yawned and had saliva shoot out your mouth, it is called gleeking. The salivary glands underneath your tongue become stimulated and shoot a concentrated jet of pure saliva; it typically happens when yawning.

750) At up to 150 pounds, the capybara from South America is the world's largest rodent.

751) The use of the word bucks for dollars dates to the 1700s when deerskins were commonly used for trading. A trade record from 1748 notes the exchange of a cask of whiskey for 5 bucks. The term stayed around after the dollar became the U.S. standard currency in 1792.

752) For centuries, families in central Europe have eaten carp for Christmas Eve dinner. In Slovakia and some nearby countries, the tradition goes further where the Christmas carp must first swim in the family bathtub for at least a day or two before being killed, cleaned and prepared.

753) You are probably pronouncing Dr. Seuss' name incorrectly. Dr. Seuss was born Theodor Seuss Geisel; Seuss was his mother's maiden name, and it is pronounced as Soice (rhymes with voice) by the family.

754) You will be the last person to die in your lifetime.

755) New Zealand has the world's steepest drivable street at a 35-degree grade.

756) During his third campaign running for president in 1912, Theodore Roosevelt delivered an 84-minute speech in Milwaukee after being shot just before the event. He was shot as he stood up in an open-air automobile and waved his hat to the crowd; fortunately, the bullet was slowed by his dense overcoat, steel-reinforced eyeglass case, and 50-page speech squeezed into his jacket pocket. X-rays taken after the speech showed the bullet lodged against Roosevelt's fourth right rib on an upward path to his heart.

757) Harry S. Truman was the first president paid a salary of $100,000 or more.

758) Rats eat their own feces for the nutritional value.

759) Mithridatism is the practice of trying to protect yourself against poisoning by taking non-lethal doses of poison to build immunity. From the end of the 1st century, Roman emperors adopted the daily habit of taking a small amount of every known poison in an attempt to gain immunity. It can be effective against some types of poisons, but depending on the poison, it can lead to a lethal accumulation in the body over time.

760) The word therein contains 10 words without rearranging any letters: the, there, he, in, rein, her, here, ere, therein, herein.

761) The acnestis is the part of an animal's skin that it can't scratch itself, usually the area between the shoulder blades.

762) In 1913, Adolf Hitler, Sigmund Freud, Marshal Tito, Leon Trotsky, and Joseph Stalin all lived in Vienna within walking distance of each other.

763) The United Kingdom has more tornadoes per square mile than any other country.

764) Theodore Roosevelt had a pet hyena named Bill which was a present from the Emperor of Ethiopia.

765) Thanks to the television series *MacGyver* that ran from 1985 until 1992 and was revived in 2016, the word MacGyver was added to the Oxford English Dictionary in 2015. As a verb, it means to make or repair an object in an improvised or inventive way, making use of whatever items are at hand.

766) By area, Saudi Arabia is the largest country that doesn't have any natural rivers; it is the 12th largest country.

767) North Korea has the highest percent of its population in the military. Between active, reserves, and paramilitary, 30.8% of the entire population is in the military. Comparatively, 0.7% of the U.S. population is in the military.

768) Austrian psychologist Julius Wagner-Jauregg won the 1927 Nobel Prize for Medicine for curing syphilis by giving people malaria. In the first half of the 20th century, it was found that certain medical conditions could be cured by creating a fever in the patient; this was known as pyrotherapy. Wagner-Jauregg was experimenting with the treatment of mental illness by induced fever; he was working with patients with dementia paralytica caused by syphilis and found that fever could cure the syphilis. He used the least aggressive malaria parasite since it produced long, high fevers. The treatment was dangerous killing up to 15% of patients, but syphilis at the time was a terminal disease, and it was viewed as an acceptable risk since malaria could later be treated with quinine.

769) Rats don't sweat; they regulate their temperature by constricting or expanding blood vessels in their tails.

770) Spraint is the dung of an otter.

771) As a mosquito sucks your blood, they also pee on you. Mosquitoes need to get rid of excess fluid and salts as they suck blood, so they urinate to maintain their fluid and salt balance.

772) A group of ravens is called an unkindness or conspiracy.

773) Horses have a single toe like other equines such as zebras and donkeys, but their ancient ancestors that lived 55 million years ago were dog like in size and had 14 toes, four toes on their front feet and three on their back.,

774) According to recent studies, there may be about one trillion species of microbes, and 99.999% of them have yet to be discovered.

775) Until 2011, Russia legally defined any beverage containing less than 10% alcohol a foodstuff, so beer was considered a soft drink.

776) Bulls don't see red. Cows, including bulls, are generally red-green colorblind; they are reacting to the motion of the fabric and not the color.

777) Maryland was the first state to adopt an official sport; they named jousting as their official sport in 1962.

778) Most East Asians and almost all Korean people don't have underarm odor. A genetic mutation called ABCC11 determines whether people produce underarm odor; people who have the ABCC11 mutation still produce sweat, but they lack a chemical that creates the smell when sweat is broken down by bacteria. While only 2% of Europeans have the mutation, over 99% of Koreans have it.

779) CarRentals.com, CheapTickets, Expedia.com, HomeAway, Hotels.com, Hotwire.com, Orbitz, Travelocity, and Trivago are all owned by the same company, Expedia Group.

780) When you die, there are companies that will put your ashes in fireworks, so you can go out with a bang.

781) As much as 95% of all dreams are forgotten shortly after waking. Research suggests that the changes in the brain during sleep do not support the information processing and storage for forming long lasting memories.

782) Virtually all barramundi fish are born male and turn into females after two years.

783) Almost 100% of Iceland's domestic electricity production is from renewable sources, and about 85% of its overall energy consumption is from renewable sources, the highest of any country.

784) Hippo milk is bright pink. Hippos secrete two unique acids, hipposudoric acid and norhipposudoric acid, that function as a natural sunscreen and antimicrobial agent. The acids are red and orange in color, and when mixed with a hippo mother's milk, they turn it bright pink.

785) The termite queen is the longest living insect. They have been known to live for at least 50 years, and some scientists believe they may live to 100.

786) Dogs tend to wag their tails more towards their right when they are relaxed and more to their left when they are afraid or insecure.

787) Because of the severe damage caused by rabbits in Australia, it is illegal to own a pet rabbit for private purposes in Queensland, Australia. You can only have a rabbit for public entertainment like magic or for science and research.

788) While on an African safari in 1954, Ernest Hemingway survived two plane crashes in two days.

789) More than half the world's population lives within a 2,500-mile diameter circle in southeastern Asia. The circle incorporates 19 countries and 22 of the 37 cities in the world with 10 million or more population.

790) About 1 in 8 American workers have worked at McDonald's at some point in their life.

791) The letter j is the only letter that doesn't appear in the periodic table of elements.

792) The term fired as in "get fired" or "you're fired" comes from the historical practice of burning down the dwelling place of unwanted members of a community who then would have no choice but to leave and would potentially not survive.

793) Natiform describes something that resembles a butt.

794) Lettuce is a member of the sunflower family.

795) Thomas Jefferson did not like public speaking and preferred to remain quiet most of the time. He only made two speeches during his entire eight-year presidency, and they were both inaugural speeches and were hardly audible.

796) Male horses have more teeth than females. Males typically have 40 teeth; females have 36; the difference is that males usually have four canine teeth which are located between the front incisors and the cheek teeth; females don't usually have canine teeth.

797) Early versions of the computer mouse were referred to as a turtle rather than a mouse presumably because of its hard shell on top.

798) The Big Dipper isn't a constellation; it is an asterism. There are 88 official constellations in the night sky; any other grouping of stars that isn't one of the 88 is an asterism. In the Big Dipper's case, it is part of the Ursa Major or Great Bear constellation.

799) It wasn't until the Indian Citizenship Act of 1924 that Native Americans were granted full United States citizenship. The act was passed partially in recognition of the thousands of Native Americans who had served in the military during WWI. The 14th amendment to the U.S. Constitution defines a citizen as any person born in the U.S. and subject to its jurisdiction, but the amendment had been interpreted to not apply to Native Americans.

800) Since the British Centurion tank was introduced in 1945, all British tanks and most armored fighting vehicles come equipped with tea making facilities. The equipment is known as a boiling vessel and draws its power from the tank's main electrical supply; it can make tea and boil water and heat food.

801) The first eight packs of Crayola crayons were sold door to door in 1903 for a nickel. The creators felt they wouldn't appeal to artists due to their poor paper adhesion, so they decided to market to children and educators.

802) The black kite, whistling kite, and brown falcon are Australian birds of prey that intentionally spread fires. Aborigines have known this for centuries, and scientists have now confirmed it. These birds hang out around the edges of fires looking for escaping prey, and they will also pick up smoldering debris and fly up to a kilometer away and drop it to spread the fire. The act appears to be very intentional to create a new area where they can wait for prey escaping the fire.

803) Because of the speed the Sun moves, the maximum possible length for a solar eclipse is 7 minutes and 58 seconds.

804) In ancient Rome, gladiators were huge celebrities; wealthy women would buy vials of their sweat and use it as face cream.

805) Research indicates that everyone dreams whether they remember doing so or not.

806) The concept of giving a key to the city comes from medieval times where walled cities were locked at night, but someone with the key could come and go as they liked.

807) Of the 10 tallest statues in the world, six are Buddhist statues.

808) Future *Today Show* weatherman Willard Scott was the first person to play Ronald McDonald in three 1963 television advertisements. Scott was a local radio personality in Washington, D.C. and had played Bozo the Clown on television from 1959-1962.

809) The earliest woodblock-printed paper book is the Chinese book *Diamond Sutra*, which was created in 868, almost 600 years before the Gutenberg Bible was the first book printed on a mechanical press.

810) In humans, our two nostrils smell differently. Odors coming in through the right nostril are judged to be more pleasant, and you can describe odors coming in through your left nostril better. The difference is believed to be due to the right nostril being connected to the right brain which deals more with emotions, and the left nostril being connected to the left brain which deals more with language.

811) Adult cats spend up to 50% of their waking time grooming.

812) An ambigram is a word, art form or other symbolic representation whose elements retain meaning when viewed or interpreted from a different direction, perspective, or orientation. For example, the word "swims" is the same when it is rotated 180 degrees.

813) If you sneeze while driving at 60 mph, your eyes are closed for about 50 feet.

814) Dolphins call each other by name. Scientists have found evidence that dolphins use a unique whistle to identify each other.

815) If you could fold an average thickness (0.004 inch) paper in half 42 times, it would be thick enough to reach the Moon; if you could fold it 103 times, it would be 109 billion light-years thick, thicker than the observable universe is wide.

816) The world record for a human going without sleep was set by 17-year-old Randy Gardner in 1964; he was intentionally awake for 11 days 25 minutes without any stimulants.

817) There is no cellphone or Wi-Fi service in Green Bank, West Virginia because it could interfere with the operation of the National Radio Astronomy Observatory's radio telescope. The National Radio Quiet Zone was created in 1958 as an area in which radio transmissions are heavily restricted by law; it covers a 13,000 square mile area straddling West Virginia's border with Virginia and Maryland. Restrictions apply to the entire area, but they are most severe the closer you get to the Green Bank Observatory.

818) The philtrum is the groove in your upper lip that runs from the top of the lip to the nose.

819) Walking takes about 200 muscles to take a single step.

820) Gorillas are several times stronger than humans; a male silverback gorilla can lift 1,800 pounds.

821) Velociraptors were nothing like they were portrayed in the movie *Jurassic Park*. They were about 3 feet tall and 6 feet overall with tail and weighed about 30 pounds, the size of a large turkey, and had feathers.

822) "In God We Trust" did not become the official U.S. national motto until 1956.

823) The name M&M's stands for Mars & Murrie, the co-creators of the candy. Forest Mars, son of the Mars candy company founder, and Bruce Murrie, son of the founder of Hershey's, went into business together in 1941 to develop the candy. M&M's contained Hershey's chocolate until 1949 when the partners had a falling out, and Mars bought back Murrie's share of the business.

824) Rich Uncle Pennybags is the mascot depicted as a portly older man with a moustache, suit, bowtie and top hat in the game Monopoly. He was inspired by tycoon J.P. Morgan. The character in jail is named Jake the Jailbird, and the police officer who sent him there is Officer Mallory.

825) American savant Kim Peek was the inspiration for the movie *Rain Man*; among his many abilities, he could read two pages of a book simultaneously. His left eye read the left page, and his right eye read the right page. Scans of his brain indicated that he didn't have the normal connections that transfer information between the left and right hemispheres which may be the reason for some of his abilities.

826) Along with murdering his own mother and his first two wives, Roman emperor Nero married a boy slave named Sporus who was designated to be a puer delicatus who were chosen as slaves of important Roman citizens because of their beauty. Nero freed Sporus and married him; he also had him castrated as was customary with puer delicatus, so his boyish looks wouldn't change. Sporus was Nero's formal wife in the eyes of everyone and dressed as an empress.

827) The green sea slug, Elysia chlorotica, which lives off the east coast of the U.S. is the first animal ever discovered that is also part plant. The slugs take chloroplasts into their skin which turns them emerald green and makes them capable of photosynthesis. They can go without eating for nine months or more, photosynthesizing as they bask in the sun.

828) If the salt in the oceans was removed and spread evenly over the Earth's land surface, it would form a layer more than 500 feet thick.

829) Antepenultimate means the third to last thing.

830) Baby porcupines are called porcupettes.

831) John F. Kennedy had a lifelong struggle with back pain and was wearing a tightly laced back brace that may have kept him from recoiling to the floor of his car after he was hit with the first bullet to the neck and made him an easier target for the second shot. The brace

was a firmly bound corset around his hips and lower back and higher up; he tightly laced it and put a wide Ace bandage in a figure eight around his trunk, so his movement was significantly restricted.

832) Australia's coastline is over 16,000 miles long and has over 10,000 beaches, more beaches than any other country in the world.

833) At the population density of New York City, the entire population of the world would fit in an area 9% larger than the state of Texas.

834) Glass is neither a liquid nor a solid; it is an amorphous solid, a state somewhere between those two states of matter.

835) Columella nasi is the fleshy end of your nose that splits your nostrils.

836) When Colgate started mass producing its toothpaste in 1873, it was in a jar; they didn't put it in tubes until the 1890s.

837) As is often the case, the Disney film *Pinocchio* was a much lighter take on the original story. The original does feature a talking cricket although he isn't named Jiminy Cricket, but Pinocchio gets mad and kills the cricket after receiving some advice he doesn't like. The talking cricket returns later as a ghost to give Pinocchio additional advice.

838) *Peyton Place* (1964-1969) was the first U.S. primetime television soap opera.

839) Dung beetles can navigate based on the position of the Moon, Sun, and stars. Researchers have found that they take a mental snapshot of the night sky and use it to find their way around. The beetles can recall their exact position based on the location of the Moon, the Sun and stars, and when presented with an artificial sky, they change their course accordingly to match.

840) Franklin D. Roosevelt was the first U.S. president to be televised while at the opening ceremonies of the 1939 New York World's Fair.

841) The creature that most people identify as a daddy long legs spider is not a spider at all; it is a long-legged harvestmen which is an

arachnid but not a spider. Harvestmen have one body section instead of the two spiders have, two eyes instead of eight, a segmented body instead of unsegmented in spiders, no silk, no venom, and a totally different respiratory system than spiders among other differences.

842) In August 1864, Abraham Lincoln was riding a horse to the Soldiers' Home outside of Washington D.C. where the president and his family stayed to escape the heat during the summer. There was a gunshot, and his horse bolted; Lincoln lost his hat which he believed was due to his horse jerking. When they went back to find his hat, they found a bullet hole in it, so there was an assassination attempt about eight months before John Wilkes Booth would assassinate Lincoln.

843) A domestic cat can't focus clearly on anything closer than about a foot away.

844) When you peel a banana, the strings that come off are called phloem bundles; the strings distribute nutrients up and down the banana as it grows.

845) Ngerulmud, Palau is the smallest population national capital in the world with less than 400 residents. Palau is an island nation in the Pacific Ocean.

846) You never have been and never will be in the same physical location twice since the Earth, our solar system, and our galaxy are all moving through space.

847) Starfish don't have blood; their circulatory system is primarily made of sea water.

848) It is estimated that 5-6 billion Bibles have been printed throughout history.

849) In terms of gross tonnage or cargo carrying capacity, the largest current cruise ships are about five times the size of the *Titanic*.

850) About 70% of the atmospheric oxygen we breathe is produced by ocean plants, mainly by phytoplankton.

851) Because of the effect temperature has on how a tennis ball bounces, all 50,000 plus balls used for a Wimbledon tournament are kept at a constant 68 degrees Fahrenheit.

852) India spends more time reading than any other country. Its citizens reported an average of 10 hours 42 minutes per week reading.

853) 111,111,111 multiplied by 111,111,111 equals 12,345,678,987,654,321.

854) During WWII, Private Wojtek in the Polish army carried ammunition to the frontline and was later promoted to corporal; he was a bear. He was also taught to salute.

855) Ancient gladiators were mainly vegetarian; their diet was grain-based and mostly meat free.

856) Toilet water in the Southern Hemisphere does not rotate in the opposite direction compared to the Northern Hemisphere due to the Coriolis effect. The Coriolis force is a real effect and is why large systems like hurricanes do rotate in different directions in the two hemispheres, but it is proportional to velocity, and its effect on a toilet flushing is miniscule compared to the water jets and other irregularities.

857) Nepetalactone, the essential oil in catnip that gives the plant its characteristic odor, is about 10 times more effective at repelling mosquitoes than DEET, the compound found in most commercial insect repellents.

858) The first regular character on U.S. television who was a divorcee was Vivian Bagley on *The Lucy Show* in 1962.

859) Blood donors in Sweden receive a text each time their blood is used.

860) Hans Island is in the middle of the Arctic and is claimed by both Canada and Denmark. The two countries periodically send a military mission to dismantle the other's flagpole and erect their own and leave a bottle of Canadian whiskey or Danish schnapps for the other.

861) Phytophotodermatitis, also known as margarita photodermatitis, is a condition you can get if you spend too much time in the sun after handling limes, lemons, or other plants containing a chemical compound called furanocoumarin. The compound in contact with exposed skin and sunlight creates a phototoxic reaction that looks and feels like a second-degree burn.

862) When touching and microwaved, two whole grapes or a pair of beads made mostly of water concentrate the energy from the microwaves at the point where they make contact and generate a very small hot spot intense enough to spark and generate plasma. The effect seems to be dependent on the size, composition, and shape of the objects.

863) In humans, night owls tend to have higher IQs, be more creative, and are mentally alert for a longer portion of the day than early birds.

864) In modern times, the first anti-smoking campaign ever was launched by the Nazis. Hitler had been a heavy smoker in his twenties, but he later condemned it as "the wrath of the Red Man against the White Man, vengeance for having been given hard liquor." It also played into the Third Reich's propaganda which labeled tobacco as genetic poison that would corrupt the German purity.

865) Christopher Columbus' three ships weren't likely called the Nina, Pinta, and Santa Maria. In the 15th century, most sailing ships were named after saints, so the Santa Maria is likely the real name, but the Nina and the Pinta were probably sailor nicknames. The Nina's real name was most likely the Santa Clara; the Pinta's real name is unknown.

866) The primary reason dog noses are wet is because dogs secrete a mucus that aids their sense of smell.

867) Kangaroos continue to grow until they die.

868) At an area of 43 square miles, Disney World is about the same size as the city of San Francisco.

869) A gallon of gasoline contains about 31,000 calories; if you could drink gasoline as fuel, you could ride a bicycle at 15 mph for about 912 miles on a gallon of gas.

870) The sound when you snap your finger is from the finger hitting the palm; it doesn't come from the finger rubbing the thumb.

871) Some expensive perfumes still contain whale poop. Ambergris, a waxy substance produced in the intestines of sperm whales, has been incorporated in perfumes for a long time as a binding agent to help the fragrances linger on the skin and intensify the scent of the perfume. It has now been mostly replaced by synthetic alternatives.

872) Casanova's first profession was a lawyer; he started college at the age of 12 and graduated with a law degree at 17.

873) Ancient Romans had a sewer goddess (Cloacina) a toilet god (Crepitus who was also the god of flatulence), and an excrement god (Stercutius).

874) Graham crackers are named after 19th century evangelical minister Sylvester Graham; he believed that food influenced libido, so he advised a bland diet to suppress lust. He espoused a coarsely ground wheat flour which became known as graham flour which later gave graham crackers their name.

875) There are far more fake flamingos in the world than there are real ones. There are just under 2 million flamingos in the wild; there are many millions of plastic ones.

876) At some points in history, money was designed to discourage people from having too much. According to Greek historian Plutarch, the Spartans used long, heavy iron rods as their currency to discourage people from pursuing great wealth. The currency was called obeloi and was so cumbersome that carrying multiple pieces would require help.

877) Trees can tell if a deer is trying to eat them and defend themselves by producing astringent tannins that taste bad and put the deer off. When a bud is damaged, the tree can sense the animal's saliva in the

wound which triggers a hormone that causes it to increase the concentration of tannins in that part of the tree. It also spurs the tree to produce more growth hormones that cause the remaining buds to grow more vigorously and make up for those that have been lost to the deer.

878) An adult blue whale's tongue weighs about 6,000–8,000 pounds or about the same as a small elephant.

879) The Brannock Device is the device they use to measure your foot at a shoe store.

880) The Earth receives more energy from the Sun every hour than the entire world uses in a year. The Earth receives about 430 quintillion joules of energy every hour from the Sun, and we use about 410 quintillion joules of energy worldwide each year.

881) About 98% of all the atoms in a human body are replaced every year.

882) Sea otters have the densest fur of all animals; they have up to one million hairs per square inch on the densest parts of their bodies.

883) The largest private home ever built in the U.S. is the Biltmore Estate in Asheville, North Carolina which was built for George Washington Vanderbilt II and was completed in 1895; it is 175,856 square feet.

884) When glass breaks, the cracks move at speeds up to 3,000 mph.

885) A second is called a second because it was the second division of the hour; the original term was second minute.

886) Despite being a ruthless warlord, Genghis Khan was very enlightened in his cultural and political policies as a ruler. He established freedom of religion, banned torture of prisoners, outlawed slavery, promoted people based on individual merit rather than birth, established universal law, created a writing system, instituted an international postal system, and redistributed the wealth he gained.

887) The Roe River in Montana is recognized as the world's shortest river; it flows for 200 feet between Giant Springs and the Missouri River near Great Falls, Montana.

888) Wendy's hamburgers are square because founder Dave Thomas took the phrase "not cutting corners" seriously, and he wanted the burgers to be square because the patties stick out of the bun in a way that showcases the meat's quality.

889) Your fingers don't contain any muscles. The muscles which bend the finger joints are in the palm and mid forearm and are connected to the finger bones by tendons which pull on and move the fingers.

890) The ancient Greeks drank their wine diluted; it was usually mixed three parts water to one part wine. If you drank undiluted wine, you were considered a drunkard and someone who lacked restraint and principle.

891) Bubble wrap was invented in 1957 by sealing two shower curtains together with some air pockets between; it was originally intended to be used as wallpaper.

892) There are an estimated 10,000,000,000,000,000,000 (10 quintillion) insects alive at any given time.

893) California's name comes from the Spanish legend of Queen Califa who ruled an island called California. When Cortéz landed in Baja California, he believed he had found the island of Queen Califa which was supposed to be populated only by women who used gold to make tools and weapons.

894) Ancient Romans ran cold aqueduct water in pipes through their houses in an early form of air conditioning.

895) The Pentagon, headquarters for the United State Department of Defense, was originally designed to fit on a piece of land that was bordered on five sides by roads. It was decided that the original site was too close to Arlington Cemetery, so it was moved to its current location. Since the design was already complete; it was slightly

modified but kept its pentagon shape even though it wasn't essential any longer.

896) In April 1933, Amelia Earhart and Eleanor Roosevelt snuck out of a White House event and commandeered an airplane and went on a joyride.

897) President Andrew Johnson was an indentured servant as a child. When he was three years old, his father passed away, and Johnson and his brother became indentured servants to a tailor; they worked for food and lodging. They both eventually ran away, and Johnson taught himself to read and worked as a tailor to support himself.

898) Most of the wasabi served outside of Japan is a mixture of horseradish, mustard and food coloring. Real wasabi is very expensive and is often not used even in Japan.

899) The word fizzle originally meant "to break wind quietly."

900) Recent research has shown that the phrase "bloodcurdling" is physically accurate. The phrase can be traced back to medieval times when people believed that being scared could make your blood run cold or congeal. Studies have now shown that watching a horror film produces a significant increase in a blood clotting protein. If you are frightened, the body seems to prepare itself for the possibility of blood loss.

# Facts 901-1200

901) In 1799 in North Carolina, a 12-year-old boy found a 17-pound gold nugget in a creek and took it home; not realizing what it was, the family used it as a doorstop for three years. In 1802, the boy's father sold the nugget to a jeweler still not realizing what it was. Later, he learned the value of the nugget which started the Carolina Gold Rush, the first in the United States.

902) While the United States represents about 4.4% of the world's population, it houses about 22% of the world's prisoners.

903) If Walmart was a country, its revenues would rank it as the 25th largest economy in the world.

904) In 1799 when he died, George Washington's distillery produced nearly 11,000 gallons, making it one of the largest whiskey distilleries in America at the time.

905) Wild chimpanzees in Guinea drink fermented palm sap which contains up to 6.9% alcohol. Some of the chimpanzees consume significant quantities and exhibit signs of inebriation.

906) Due to a shortage of space in London to bury people, the London Necropolis Railway line was opened in 1854 to carry corpses and mourners between London and the Brookwood Cemetery 23 miles southwest of London. At the time, it was the largest cemetery in the world and was designed to accommodate all London deaths for centuries. The station waiting rooms and the train compartments for both living and dead passengers were partitioned by religion and class to prevent mixing mourners and cadavers from different social backgrounds. By 1941, slightly over 200,000 burials had been conducted in the cemetery, which was far fewer than planned, and the railway line wasn't used again after being damaged during WWII.

907) In the Humpty Dumpty nursery rhyme, there is no indication that he is an egg. Early illustrations portrayed him as a young boy.

908) The Canadian province of Alberta is the largest rat free populated area in the world. The government has had very aggressive rat control measures since the 1950s, and only the brown rat is capable of surviving in the prairie region and must still overwinter in buildings.

909) The practice of quarantine began during the 14th century when ships arriving in Venice from plague infected ports were required to sit at anchor for 40 days before landing. The word quarantine derives from the Italian words "quaranta giorni" which mean 40 days.

910) NASA accidentally erased and reused the original 1969 Moon landing tapes from *Apollo 11*. The tapes were reused as part of a money saving effort.

911) In the 1st century, the Romans had polar bears fight seals in amphitheaters they flooded with water.

912) Along with other benefits, a U.S. Medal of Honor recipient gets a retired pay increase of 10%, a special Medal of Honor pension of over $1,300 per month above and beyond any other benefits, a special supplemental clothing allowance, and free lifelong travel on Department of Defense military aircraft.

913) You can't really cry in space because there isn't gravity for tears to flow downward. The liquid builds up in a ball in the eye until it is large enough to break free of the eye and float around.

914) A jellyfish's mouth also serves as its anus.

915) The only two countries where Coca-Cola isn't sold are Cuba and North Korea.

916) Even though the human sense of smell is not near as sophisticated as some animals, recent research estimates that the human nose can detect at least 1 trillion different scents.

917) Worldwide, there are about 107 human deaths per minute or about 1.78 deaths per second.

918) Due to anti-German sentiment during WWI, the British royal family chose to change their name to Windsor from Saxe-Coburg and Gotha in 1917, so the family is named after the castle and not the other way around.

919) In space, blood flow doesn't work the same without gravity. Blood can flow up towards the head instead of pulling down toward the feet. Astronaut's faces typically look puffy from extra blood flow for the first few days until their bodies adapt.

920) Writing punctuation as we largely know it today did not exist until the 15th century.

921) Ninety percent of all English written material is made up of just 1,000 words.

922) The average human worldwide weighs about 137 pounds.

923) Rome, Italy is located at about the same latitude as the southernmost point of Canada and is farther north than 62% of the United States by area.

924) From the 1920s until the 1970s before the risk of x-rays was well understood, shoe shops used x-ray machines for shoe fittings in the United States, Canada, United Kingdom, South Africa, Germany and Switzerland. The device had an opening where the customer would place their feet and while standing would look through a viewing window at the top to see the x-ray view of their feet and shoes. There were typically two other viewing windows on either side to allow a parent and sales assistant to look at the fit. The bones of the feet, outline of the shoe, and stitching around the edges were clearly visible.

925) The Amazon rainforest is home to 10% of the known species in the world.

926) The Pacific Ocean side entrance to the Panama Canal is further east than the Atlantic Ocean side entrance.

927) About 1850 BC, the earliest known contraceptive devices for women were invented. They were objects or concoctions inserted into the vagina to block or kill sperm; Egyptians used concoctions made of crocodile dung, honey, and sodium carbonate.

928) Jane Addams was the first American woman to win a Nobel Prize; she shared the Nobel Peace Prize in 1931.

929) An ostrich's eye is bigger than its brain.

930) In 1898, Morgan Robertson wrote a short novel called *Futility* about a large unsinkable ship called the *Titan* which carried an insufficient number of lifeboats, and on an April voyage, it hits an iceberg and sinks in the North Atlantic resulting in the loss of almost everyone on board. Fourteen years later in April 1912, the large unsinkable *Titanic* with an insufficient number of lifeboats hit an iceberg and sank in the North Atlantic losing most of the people on board.

931) Kodak created the first digital still camera in 1975; it weighed 8 pounds and took 0.01-megapixel black-and-white photos that took 23 seconds to render onto a cassette tape that displayed the image on a television set.

932) Stephen Girard was one of the wealthiest men in American history, and he personally saved the U.S. from financial collapse during the War of 1812 by placing most of his personal assets at the disposal of the government and underwriting about 95% of the war loans.

933) Bookkeeper and bookkeeping are the only two English words with three consecutive double letters.

934) It would take about 150 ruby-throated hummingbirds to weigh one pound.

935) Baby elephants suck their trunk for comfort just like human babies suck their thumb.

936) Three dogs survived the *Titanic* sinking, a Pekinese and two Pomeranians.

937) In France, most toilet paper sold for use in the home is pink.

938) The Titanoboa is the largest snake ever known to have existed; it lived about 60 million years ago and was up to 42 feet long and weighed up to 2,500 pounds.

939) There are 2.3 billion square feet of rental self-storage in the United States, and almost 10% of households rent storage at an average monthly cost of $91.

940) In 1988, presidential nominee George Bush considered bringing on Clint Eastwood as his running mate.

941) In 1980, the world's first 1 gigabyte disk drive took up the space of a refrigerator, weighed 1,000 pounds, and cost $81,000.

942) Located in Fez, Morocco, the al-Qarawiyyin library is the world's oldest working library operating since 859 AD.

943) King Tut's tomb had already been robbed several times before it was discovered by Howard Carter in 1922.

944) Flamingos are naturally white; their brine shrimp and algae diet makes them pink.

945) Cornicione is name for the outer part of a pizza crust.

946) The Jeep name comes from the army where "general purpose" was abbreviated as G.P. which phonetically translates to Jeep.

947) In the 1600s, some doctors recommended their patients fart into jars and store it to later inhale to ward off the bubonic plague. The idea was that the plague was caused by deadly vapors, so it could be warded off by foul vapors.

948) Nearly half the world's population are lifetime abstainers of alcohol.

949) A mononymous person is known and addressed by one name.

950) Flamingos bend their legs at the ankle and not the knee. Their knee is located much higher up hidden under their feathers. The whole area from the ankle to the toes is a giant foot; the joint that looks like an ankle near the bottom of their leg is the beginning of their toes, so about half of what appears to be the flamingo's legs are really its feet.

951) When the first tea bags were developed, the idea was that customers would remove the tea from the bags, but they preferred to brew the tea in the bag.

952) Ketchup originated in China many centuries ago; the original sauce was derived from fermented fish. The British picked it up and altered it to be more like a Worcestershire sauce. Tomatoes weren't used in ketchup until the early 19th century in the United States.

953) It takes about 1,000 years for any cubic meter of ocean water to circulate around the world.

954) Early Americans used corn cobs for toilet paper. Dried corncobs were plentiful, efficient, and are softer and more flexible than you think.

955) Written out in English (one, two, three, etc.), eight is the first number alphabetically no matter how high you go.

956) The expression "worth one's salt" originated in ancient Rome where soldiers were sometimes paid in salt or given an allowance to purchase it. The word salary derives from the Latin "salarium" referring to a soldier's allowance to buy salt.

957) Birds are essentially immune to the heat of chili peppers; they don't have the right type or number of taste receptors to be affected.

958) Snapping shrimp can snap their specialized claw shut producing a cavitation bubble that releases a sound as loud as 218 decibels, louder

than a rocket launch. When the bubble collapses, it can reach temperatures of 4,700 degrees Celsius, almost as hot as the surface of the Sun which is 5,500 degrees Celsius.

959) Albert Einstein described it as "spooky action at a distance" and didn't believe nature would be so unreasonable, but the idea of quantum entanglement that occurs when two particles are inextricably linked together no matter their physical separation has been proven repeatedly in experiments. Although entangled particles are not physically connected, they are still able to share information with each other instantaneously breaking the rule that no information can be transmitted faster than the speed of light. Entangled particles 750 miles apart have shown that any change in one is instantly reflected in the other; this would be true even if they were separated by light-years.

960) The Motel 6 and Super 8 motel chains both got their names from their original room rates. Motel 6 charged $6 per night when it started in 1962, and Super 8 charged $8.88 per night when it started in 1974.

961) Using a thin, flexible sheet of plastic, scientists have created a device that can collect electricity from snowfall. Snow is positively charged and gives up electrons; silicone is negatively charged and accepts the electrons. As snow lands on the silicone, a charge is produced and captured.

962) Lucy, a star in the constellation Centaurus 50 light-years away, is about 90% crystalized carbon making it a huge 10 billion trillion trillion carat diamond.

963) If you average out the colors of all the different stars we can see, you get beige, so the average color of the observable universe is beige.

964) There are an estimated one million spiders per acre of land; in the tropics, there are closer to three million per acre.

965) Captain Morgan rum is named after the 17th century Welsh privateer Sir Henry Morgan. A privateer is essentially a pirate who is

sanctioned by the government; he was hired by the British to protect their interests in the Caribbean from the Spanish.

966) Speed dating was created by Jewish Rabbi Yaacov Deyo in 1998. At a Beverly Hills, California matchmaking event, he brought along a gragger, the noisemaker Jews use during Purim; he twirled the gragger when it was time to switch partners. They decided on 10 minutes for each date because it was an easy number.

967) Canadian law requires that a skill testing element must be included for a sweepstakes to be legal. A sweepstakes winner cannot be determined by pure luck; there must be some skill involved. The skill test is often a mathematical test involving some combination of addition, subtraction, multiplication, and division that must be performed without a calculator or other aid.

968) You can fire a gun in the oxygen free environment of space. Fires can't burn without oxygen, but modern ammunition contains its own oxidizer to trigger the explosion of gunpowder and fire the bullet; no atmospheric oxygen is required.

969) Tic Tacs were introduced in 1969 under the name Refreshing Mints; in 1970, the name was changed to Tic Tac because of the sound the mints made rattling in their container.

970) While only 3.1% of the world's children live in the United States, they own 40% of the toys consumed globally.

971) Nellie Tayloe Ross became the first female U.S. state governor in 1925; she won a special election after her husband, Governor William Ross of Wyoming, died in 1924.

972) In 1776, Margaret Corbin became the first woman recognized as a soldier in the American Revolutionary War; she was also the first woman to receive a U.S. military pension.

973) There is a southern version of the aurora borealis (northern lights) called the aurora australis which can be seen from Antarctica, New Zealand, Argentina, and Australia.

974) A nurdle is the wave-like gob of toothpaste you put on your toothbrush.

975) With 1.5 crimes per citizen, Vatican City has the highest crime rate per capita in the world. The reason is that the population is only about 800 with millions of tourists, and the crime is mainly petty theft.

976) Duncan Hines (1880–1959) was a real person; he was an American pioneer of restaurant ratings for travelers.

977) Seahorses are very bad swimmers. They propel themselves using a dorsal fin that beats 30-70 times per second. The tiny fin and an awkward body shape make it difficult to get around, and they can easily die of exhaustion navigating in stormy water.

978) Harry S. Truman was the last U.S. president without a college degree.

979) The coldest temperature ever recorded on Earth was minus 128.56 degrees Fahrenheit on July 21, 1983 at Antarctica's Vostok station.

980) Insects don't flap their wings like birds do. An insect's wings are attached to its exoskeleton; they contract their muscles and force their whole body to vibrate which causes the wings to vibrate.

981) If you have red, bloodshot eyes after swimming in a pool, it isn't chlorine causing the reaction; it is urine mixing with the pool's chemicals. The nitrogen in urine combines with the chlorine and forms chloramine which is what causes the eye irritation.

982) Dolphins are usually born tail first to minimize the risk of drowning.

983) Lipsticks, nail polishes, and cosmetic products containing pearl essence or pearlescence contain fish scales. It is a silvery substance added for its shimmer effect and is primarily sourced from herring.

984) Most streets in Japan don't have a name. Instead, blocks are given a number, and buildings or houses within the block have a number, but the house or building number is typically assigned by the order they

were built, so building number 1 might be right next to building number 13.

985) In 1869, Arabella Mansfield became the first female lawyer in America.

986) Rats are not likely to blame for transmitting the Black Death bubonic plague that wiped out one-third of Europe's population in the 14th century. Experiments assessing the transmission routes prove that the parasites that carried the disease were much more likely to have come from human fleas and lice.

987) The tufts of hair in a cat's ear are called ear furnishings; they help keep out dirt, direct sounds, and insulate the ears.

988) When feeding, a hummingbird can lick 10-15 times per second.

989) The color orange is named after the fruit and not the other way around.

990) Opossums are a great help in preventing the spread of Lyme disease. They are fastidiously clean and spend hours cleaning themselves like cats do; as they clean their fur, they pick off and swallow the ticks which kills them. Studies have shown a single opossum can destroy 5,000 ticks in a season.

991) Less than 10% of legally blind Americans can read Braille.

992) None of the Beatles could read or write music. When they needed to write music for others to play, arrangers at sheet music publishing companies would do it.

993) Ed Sullivan made the Rolling Stones sing "Let's Spend the Night Together" as "Let's Spend Some Time Together" on his television show.

994) As a defense mechanism when threatened, sea cucumbers can eviscerate themselves and shoot out their internal organs. Sea cucumbers are echinoderms which also include marine animals like starfish and sea urchins; depending on the species, they can shoot the

organs out their head or butt, but they can regrow the organs. Through a process called dedifferentiation, certain cells in their bodies lose their specialized functions and move around the sea cucumber's body and become whatever type of cell is needed to regrow the lost organs.

995) Sex is sometimes dangerous for flies. When some flies mate, they emit a buzzing sound that attracts the attention of predatory bats, so they only copulate briefly.

996) The division sign (short horizontal line with a dot above and below) in math is called an obelus.

997) The largest contiguous land empire in history was Genghis Khan's Mongol Empire which spanned 9.27 million square miles in one mass at its peak in 1270. The British Empire at its peak in 1920 was larger but scattered around the world.

998) Most Japanese schools don't employ janitors or custodians; they believe that requiring students to clean the school teaches respect, responsibility, and promotes equality.

999) Violet Jessop (1887-1971) survived the collision of the *RMS Olympic* on September 20th, 1911, the sinking of the *RMS Titanic* on April 14th, 1912, and the sinking of the *HMHS Britannic* on November 21st, 1916. She was an ocean line stewardess and nurse.

1000) New York City is further south than Rome, Italy.

1001) Queen is the only music group where every member has written more than one number one single; all four members have been inducted into the Songwriters Hall of Fame.

1002) In Boston, Massachusetts in January 1919, a 50-foot-tall holding tank burst open sending a 15-foot-tall wave of molasses through the streets. It crushed houses and killed 21 people and injured 150.

1003) Statistically, the deadliest job in America is president; four presidents have been assassinated in office which is an 8.9% fatality rate.

1004) Rin Tin Tin was born in a bombed out French village during WWI and was voted most popular film performer in the U.S. in 1926.

1005) The first time an NHL team pulled their goalie to have an extra attacker was in 1931. The Boston Bruins pulled their goalie in a playoff game against the Montreal Canadiens.

1006) Snails slide around on a single foot; the one long muscle acts like a human extremity and helps them grip and push themselves along the ground.

1007) There are about 3 trillion total trees in the world.

1008) Human babies are born without kneecaps; the cartilage in their knee ossifies into kneecaps at three to five years old.

1009) Martin Luther didn't likely dramatically nail his 95 Theses to the church door in 1517. There is no historical evidence that Luther posted the theses on the church door, and the story didn't appear until 30 years after. He did mail the 95 Theses to the archbishop; Luther was a devout Catholic, and he never intended to start a revolution; he simply wanted the clergy to recognize their corruption.

1010) Martial arts action movie star Jackie Chan is also a popstar in his native China; he is a classically trained singer who in his youth was sent to the China Drama Academy where he learned his acrobatic style of martial arts as well as singing and acting. He has produced over 20 different albums including over 100 songs in five languages and won the Best Foreign Singer Award in Japan in 1984.

1011) Quetzalcoatlus was a pterodactyloid pterosaur from the Late Cretaceous period of North America and is the largest known flying animal to have ever lived. It had a wingspan up to 36 feet and may have weighed as much as 500 pounds.

1012) Canada has a strategic maple syrup reserve to ensure global supply in the case of emergency. The reserve contains about 2.4 million gallons of syrup. Quebec province produces about 75% of the global supply of maple syrup.

1013) In 1991, *L.A. Law* had the first romantic kiss between two women on primetime U.S. television. Female characters Abby played by Michele Greene and C.J. played by Amanda Donohoe kissed.

1014) The tallest married couple ever were Canadian Anna Haining Swan who was 7'11" and American Martin Van Buren Bates who was 7'9". The couple were married in 1871, and Swan later gave birth to a 22-pound baby.

1015) Snail slime is mucus which lubricates the surface and helps them move faster with less friction; they often travel in the mucus trails of other snails to move faster.

1016) Movie trailers originally played after the movie which is why they were called trailers.

1017) Jaywalker originated because jay used to be a term for an idiot or simpleton and was often applied to rural people; to jay walk was to be stupid and ignore signs and cross the street in an unsafe place.

1018) The average American professional football game lasts 3 hours and 12 minutes but only has about 11 minutes when the ball is in play.

1019) According to research, cannibalism for some animals such as certain fish, reptiles, and amphibians may be a way to help their offspring survive when overcrowding becomes a problem.

1020) If you measure from base to summit, Hawaii's Mauna Kea is the tallest mountain in the world. Measured from the seafloor where it starts, Mauna Kea is about 33,500 feet tall, almost 4,500 feet taller than Mount Everest, but it only reaches 13,796 feet above sea level.

1021) Crocodiles and alligators can climb trees. Researchers have found adults as high as 6 feet off the ground, and juveniles have been spotted as high as 30 feet.

1022) The GPS service used around the world is paid for by American taxpayers mainly through the Department of Defense which has primary responsibility for developing and operating the system. The operational cost of the system is over $2 million per day. GPS is not the only space-based radio navigation system; Russia has GLONASS; the European Union has Galileo, and China has BeiDou.

1023) Ancient Roman public toilets had a long marble bench with holes on top where you sat and holes in front for the sponge on a stick which was used to clean yourself after. There were no doors or dividing walls; you sat right next to someone else. Once you had done your business, you would rinse the sponge in the channel of running water at your feet, push the sponge on a stick through the hole in the front and wipe yourself and then rinse off the sponge and leave it in a basin for the next person.

1024) St. Peter Stiftskulinarium restaurant in Salzburg, Austria is the oldest restaurant in the world and has been in operation since 803 AD.

1025) Eleven states have land farther south than the most northern part of Mexico - Alabama, Arizona, California, Florida, Georgia, Hawaii, Louisiana, Mississippi, New Mexico, South Carolina, and Texas.

1026) Ulage is the unfilled space between a bottle top and the liquid inside.

1027) If sound waves could travel through space like they do through air, you would hear the Sun burning at a volume of about 100 decibels, about the same volume as a chainsaw or jackhammer. Sound intensity decreases with distance, so the 93 million miles to the Sun has a large impact on the volume.

1028) The Brothers Grimm version of *Cinderella* is a much darker story; the stepsisters cut off their toe and a part of their heel to fit into the shoe, and they try to go to Cinderella's wedding and get their eyes plucked out by birds.

1029) Corn, rice, and wheat account for about 51% of the world's calorie intake.

1030) The metal part of a pencil that holds the eraser in place is called the ferrule.

1031) The geographic center of the contiguous United States is two miles northwest of the town of Lebanon, Kansas on a pig farm.

1032) You will never actually see yourself; you only see representations of yourself or a flipped image in a mirror.

1033) The United States adopted the 911 emergency phone number in 1968 with the first call being made in Haleyville, Alabama.

1034) Sharks have a very well-developed sense of hearing. Their ears are small holes on the sides of their head that lead directly to the inner ear. They are particularly good at hearing low-frequency noises such as an injured fish would make and at finding out where a noise is coming from.

1035) Dr. James Naismith, who invented the game of basketball in 1891, is the only Kansas Jayhawk men's basketball coach in history with a losing record. He founded the University of Kansas basketball program where he became the Kansas coach and athletic director.

1036) After dropping out 34 years earlier, Steven Spielberg got his Bachelor of Arts degree from Cal State Long Beach; they gave him course credit for paleontology for the work he did on *Jurassic Park*.

1037) In 1999, a federal arbitration panel decided that the U.S. government had to pay the heirs of Abraham Zapruder $16 million for his original film of President John F. Kennedy's assassination. The acquisition was necessitated by a 1992 federal law that required all records of the Kennedy assassination to be transferred to the National Archives for preservation and research. The Zapruder family still controlled licensing of images from the film; the issue was the value of the original.

1038) If you started with $0.01 and had a 100% daily return on your money, you would be a millionaire in 27 days.

1039) An adult male human loses about 96 million cells every minute which are replaced by cells dividing.

1040) In 1937, Liechtenstein added a crown to their flag after discovering at the 1936 Summer Olympics that their flag was identical to Haiti.

1041) The pineapple is a berry; it produces hundreds of flowers within a small space which produce fruits which coalesce into a single larger fruit.

1042) Built in 1884, the first official skyscraper was the Home Insurance Building in downtown Chicago. It was 10 stories and 136 feet tall and was demolished in 1931.

1043) Bread and beer were the two staples of the ancient Egyptian diet; almost everyone consumed both every day. Laborers would have a morning meal of bread, beer, and often onions, and a heartier dinner with boiled vegetables, meat, and more bread and beer.

1044) The highest and lowest points in the contiguous United States are in the same county. Mount Whitney at 14,494 feet and the Badwater Basin in Death Valley at 282 feet below sea level are separated by 85 miles in Inyo County, California.

1045) A group of butterflies is called a kaleidoscope.

1046) Queen Elizabeth II has owned more than 30 corgis.

1047) The first food ever microwaved on purpose was popcorn. In 1945, Raytheon patented the first microwave oven; engineer Percy Spencer had first discovered the heating powers of microwaves when he accidentally melted a candy bar in his pocket. He tested it out officially on popcorn which was a success and on an egg which exploded.

1048) All humans are about 99.9% genetically the same.

1049) There is a vast reservoir of water three times the volume of all the oceans about 400 miles beneath the Earth's crust. The water is locked up in a mineral called ringwoodite.

1050) An average alligator can go through 2,000 to 3,000 teeth in a lifetime. An alligator has roughly 80 teeth, and as the teeth wear down, they are replaced.

1051) On May 23, 2012, the U.S. nuclear submarine USS Miami was damaged beyond repair by a fire set by an employee to get out of work early. While it was docked in a navy shipyard for overhaul, civilian employee Casey J. Fury started the fire by igniting some rags; he was sentenced to 17 years in federal prison and ordered to pay $400 million.

1052) Lake Nicaragua in Central America is one of the very few freshwater lakes in the world with sharks. Bull sharks can survive in both fresh and saltwater and make their way back and forth from the Caribbean Sea to Lake Nicaragua via a 120-mile route though the San Juan river. Researchers have tagged sharks and verified that they move back and forth from the lake and the sea.

1053) Heat index is a measure of the discomfort the average person experiences as a result of the combined effects of air temperature and humidity. The world's highest recorded heat index was 178 at Dhahran, Saudi Arabia on July 8, 2003 with a temperature of 108 and a dew point of 95.

1054) Bananas along with other potassium rich foods like spinach, apricots, salmon, avocados, and mushrooms are radioactive. K-40 radioactive atoms make up a very small fraction of potassium atoms; they spontaneously decay releasing beta radiation and gamma rays which are both capable of tissue damage. However, K-40 is not very radioactive with a half-life of 1.3 billion years, so you would have to eat about 10 million bananas to die of radiation poisoning.

1055) An avocado doesn't ripen on the tree. They only ripen once they are off the tree, so the trees can be used as storage and will keep avocados fresh for up to seven months.

1056) The Memphis, Tennessee Bass Pro Shops Megastore is one of the largest pyramids in the world and features a hotel, indoor swamp, aquarium, bowling alley, and the world's tallest freestanding elevator. The pyramid is 321 feet tall with a 535,000 square foot interior.

1057) The male antechinus, a small mouse-like mammal in Australia, essentially kills itself mating. During their first mating season, males mate as much as 14 hours straight with as many females as they can encounter over a short three-week period. Physically, males rapidly deteriorate during the mating period and very few survive.

1058) The boa constrictor is the only living animal that has the same common and scientific name.

1059) The average pencil has enough graphite to draw a line 35 miles long or write about 45,000 words.

1060) Mount Rushmore cost less than $1 million to build; it took 14 years from 1927-1941 to construct and employed 400 people.

1061) The Appalachian Mountains used to be as tall as the Rockies but are shrinking; meanwhile, the Himalayas used to be the size of the Rockies and are growing.

1062) There are about 2.5 human births for every death in the world.

1063) The first nonstop flight across the Atlantic was in 1919, eight years before Charles Lindbergh's flight. Lindbergh was the 19th pilot to fly nonstop across the Atlantic, but he was the first to do it solo. British aviators John Alcock and Arthur Brown made the first transatlantic flight from St. John's, Newfoundland to Clifton, Ireland in June 1919.

1064) Stockholm, Sweden is built on 14 islands.

1065) After going deaf, Beethoven discovered that if he bit on a metal pole connected to the piano he was playing, he could hear almost perfectly. This process is known as bone conduction; vibrations are transferred into the bones, and the ears pick up the signal with no sound distortion bypassing the eardrums. We all hear sounds through both our bones and our eardrums; most sounds are air conducted where the eardrum converts sound waves to vibrations and transmits them to the inner ear; however, in some cases, vibrations are heard directly by the inner ear bypassing your eardrums. This is one of the ways you hear your own voice.

1066) Despite scoring 28,596 points in his NBA career, basketball great Shaquille O'Neal only made one three-point shot out of 22 attempts in his entire NBA career. His only three-point basket came on February 16, 1996 when the Orlando Magic played the Milwaukee Bucks.

1067) Napoleon Bonaparte wrote a romance novel called *Clisson et Eugénie*; it was a fictional account of the doomed romance of a soldier and his lover based on Bonaparte's own relationship with Eugenie Desiree Clary.

1068) The television Emmy awards get their name from a term commonly used for the image orthicon tube used in the early cameras which was called an immy; the name was feminized to Emmy to match the female statuette.

1069) The Fitzroy River turtle, a species that can only be found in the Fitzroy River in Australia, can breathe through its anus. They are constantly pumping water in and out of their anus collecting as much as 70% of all the oxygen they need to survive. Consequently, they can stay underwater for up to three weeks at a time. They are not the only turtle species that can breathe through its anus, but they are able to use the function to a greater extent.

1070) In 1828, Ioannis Kapodistriasthe, the first governor of Greece, spread the potato as a Greek crop by getting people to steal them. He tried to introduce potatoes as a crop to help with the Greek hunger problem, but when he offered potatoes to anyone interested, no one wanted them, so he ordered the shipment of potatoes be put on public display under guard. People assumed the potatoes must be important since they were guarded and began to steal them which the guards allowed. They took all the potatoes and spread the potato as a Greek crop.

1071) Less than 1% of dreams contain smell, taste, or pain elements. Most dreams contain visual and movement features, and half of all dreams contain auditory elements.

1072) A shark can have over 30,000 teeth in its lifetime. A shark's teeth are arranged in rows with each successive row smaller than the last. On average, they have 15 rows of teeth with some species having up to 50 rows. The row nearest the front are the largest and most used. If a shark loses a tooth, the tooth in the row behind it moves up to take its place. A shark's teeth are not embedded in its jaw; they are attached to skin covering the jaw. New teeth are continually being grown in a groove in the shark's mouth, and the skin moves the teeth forward into new positions. If they didn't have the ability to quickly replace their teeth, they wouldn't have been able to develop such a strong bite which causes them to lose so many teeth.

1073) At normal atmospheric pressure, helium is the only element in the universe that can't freeze; it can't get cold enough.

1074) On June 4, 1923, Frank Hayes was the first jockey to ride to victory after his own death. He suffered a fatal heart attack mid race at Belmont Park in New York, but he somehow remained in the saddle long enough to cross the finish line for a 20-1 long shot win.

1075) Abolitionist Frederick Douglass was the most photographed American of the 19th century. He wanted to ensure a more accurate depiction of black Americans and sat for upwards of 160 portraits.

1076) In 1890, Wyoming became the first state where women had the right to vote; it had given women the right to vote as a territory in 1869.

1077) Margaret Abbott (1878–1955) was the first American woman to win an Olympic gold medal; she won the women's golf tournament at the 1900 Paris Games.

1078) The largest waterfall in the world is underwater. The Denmark Strait cataract is located between Greenland and Iceland and is 100 miles long and drops 11,500 feet from the Greenland Sea into the Irminger Sea. It is three times taller than Angel Falls in Venezuela and has 2,000 times more water than Niagara Falls. The cataract is formed by the difference in temperature between the cold Arctic waters of the Greenland Sea and the slightly warmer Irminger Sea. When the waters meet, the colder Greenland Sea water falls to the bottom.

1079) Ostrakismos, meaning ostracism, was a procedure in ancient Greece where any citizen could be voted out and expelled for 10 years. In some instances, it was used to express popular anger against an individual, but it was often used preemptively to remove someone who was thought to be a threat to the state.

1080) Alice in Wonderland Syndrome is a neuropsychological condition where people may perceive objects to be larger or smaller than they really are or nearer or farther away than they really are and can also affect the perception of the passage of time and other senses. It is often associated with migraines, brain tumors, and psychoactive drug use.

1081) New York's Central Park is the most visited urban park in the United States, and finding your way along its long, winding paths over 843 acres can be confusing; that is why Central Park's 1,600 decorative lamp posts feature plaques with four numbers on them to help with directions. The first two numbers indicate the closest cross street, and the last two numbers indicate which side of the park the lamp is closer to. Even numbers mean the east side, and odd numbers mean west. The last two digits get larger as you get closer to the center of the park.

1082) San Francisco's cable cars and the New Orleans Saint Charles streetcar line are the only two mobile national monuments in the U.S.

1083) A bog body is a human body that has been preserved in a bog; the preservation can be extremely effective. In 1952, researchers discovered a man who lived around 300 BC that was so well-preserved they could determine his cause of death, a slit throat.

1084) In 1980, new Iraqi President Saddam Hussein was awarded the key to the city of Detroit by Mayor Coleman Young for having donated $250,000 to a local church.

1085) About half of all people can remember at least one instance of lucid dreaming where they realize they are dreaming, but they are still asleep.

1086) IKEA uses almost 1% of the world's commercial wood supply.

1087) Sewer manhole covers are round because the cover rests on a lip that is smaller than the cover so it can't fall through the opening. No matter its dimensions, a square or rectangular cover could always fall through.

1088) George Washington grew hemp at Mount Vernon for rope and canvas making.

1089) By looking at a variety of animal species, a study found that the bigger the brain an animal has the longer its yawn is.

1090) Spices come from every part of a plant other than the leaf; herbs are the leaf itself.

1091) Of the 20 most watched regular television broadcasts in U.S. history, 19 have been Super Bowl broadcasts; the only other show in the top 20 is the *M*A*S*H* series finale.

1092) Early 18th century pirate Benjamin Hornigold once attacked a merchant ship just to steal the crew member's hats; his men had gotten drunk the night before and threw their hats overboard.

1093) To get the stunning detail in his bird paintings, John James Audubon would often kill the subject and pose it, so he could create realistic paintings without the subject flying away.

1094) Franklin D. Roosevelt was the first president to name a woman to his cabinet; in 1933, he named Frances Perkins as secretary of labor.

1095) Turritopsis dohrnii, also known as the immortal jellyfish, is the only immortal creature. Once the adult jellyfish has reproduced, they transform themselves back into their juvenile state. Their tentacles retract; their bodies shrink, and they sink to the ocean floor and start their life cycle all over again. They can do it repeatedly making them essentially immortal unless they are consumed by another fish or struck by disease.

1096) John F. Kennedy was the first president to have been a Boy Scout.

1097) You can always see your nose, but you don't see it unless you think about it. The process is called unconscious selective attention and allows the brain to block out distractions.

1098) The color of an egg has nothing to do with nutrition, quality, or flavor. In general, white-feathered chickens with white earlobes lay white eggs, and reddish-brown-feathered chickens with red earlobes lay brown eggs.

1099) Cats don't have good close vision, so when they are close to water, they may not be able to see the water or the water level. That is why they will frequently paw the water to feel the level or move the dish to cause a disturbance in the water so they can see it.

1100) A rat can tread water for three days and survive being flushed down the toilet.

1101) In 2012, scientists discovered a new species of ant that appears to live exclusively in New York City. The ant was discovered where Broadway meets 63rd street and 76th street and is called the ManhattAnt. They believe it has evolved to adapt to its warmer, drier, concrete-covered environment.

1102) A contronym is a word with two opposite meanings such as clip which can mean to fasten or detach.

1103) The United States and the Soviet Union were in talks to go to the Moon together; Nikita Khrushchev was about to accept the plan proposed by John F. Kennedy when Kennedy was assassinated.

Khrushchev had built up a relationship with Kennedy and was suspicious of the new Johnson administration, so he rejected the plan.

1104) Artist Salvador Dali loved money and in his later years developed a method to avoid paying at restaurants. He would have a party out with a group and write a check for the whole meal. He would then make a drawing on the back of the check knowing that the restaurant owner would rather keep the check because of the value of the drawing rather than cashing it.

1105) If you wrapped a rope around the Earth's equator tightly hugging the ground, you would only need to add about 6.3 feet of rope for it to hover one foot above the ground all the way around the Earth.

1106) During the Cold War, Soviets could tell if a passport was fake by looking at the staples; the staples in real Soviet passports corroded quickly because of low quality metal.

1107) The United States has been at war in about 93% of the calendar years it has existed.

1108) Even though it is the exact same size, the Moon appears to be larger when it is nearer the horizon than when it is higher in the sky. This is known as the Moon Illusion and has been known since ancient times. There is no consensus on what causes the illusion, but the most important factor is likely that terrain and other objects are in view along with the Moon that impact the perception of distance and size when it is nearer the horizon.

1109) As a gas, oxygen is odorless and colorless; in its liquid and solid forms, it looks pale blue.

1110) Buddha, Confucius, and Socrates all lived about the same time. Buddha is believed to have died in 483 BC; Confucius died in 479 BC, and Socrates was born in 469 BC.

1111) The Great Barrier Reef is the largest living structure on Earth. Situated off the northeastern coast of Australia, it stretches for 1,429 miles and covers an area of approximately 133,000 square miles.

1112) The longest English word in any major dictionary is the 45 letter pneumonoultramicroscopicsilicovolcanoconiosis which is a lung disease caused by inhalation of silicate or quartz dust.

1113) The first automatically sliced commercial bread was produced in 1928 in Missouri.

1114) In 1920, Babe Ruth alone hit more home runs than any other entire American League team.

1115) The sword-billed hummingbird is the only bird with a bill longer than its body.

1116) Blood can be used as an egg substitute in cooking. Blood and eggs have a similar protein composition particularly with the albumin that gives both their coagulant properties. In tests, 65 grams of blood substituted for one egg.

1117) In a show of dominance, male Indian rhinos can spray urine over 16 feet; this is typically done in the presence of other males or breeding-age females.

1118) It takes about 90 minutes to hard boil an ostrich egg.

1119) When playing with female puppies, male puppies will often let the female win even if they have a physical advantage.

1120) Circus Maximus, the ancient Roman venue for chariot racing, could seat 250,000 spectators. The track was 540 meters long by 80 meters wide and had 12 starting gates for chariots. It was constructed in the 6th century BC, and the last chariot races were held there in the 6th century AD.

1121) In 1999, NASA estimated that antimatter cost $62.5 trillion per gram or $28 quadrillion per pound to produce.

1122) Louis Armstrong was so hard on his lips with his trumpet playing that he developed lip callouses that he treated with a special salve or even removed himself using a razor blade. Satchmo's Syndrome is named after Armstrong and is a disorder due to the rupture of orbicularis oris muscle in the mouth typically in trumpet players.

1123) Ben & Jerry learned how to make ice cream by taking a $5 correspondence course offered by Penn State.

1124) Bumblebees have been found at altitudes as high as 18,000 feet, and tests have shown that they can fly at over 29,000 feet.

1125) The Greek national anthem "Hymn to Liberty" has 158 verses. The anthem is a poem by Dionysios Solomos written in 1823 and set to music by Nikolaos Mantzaros; it is the longest national anthem in the world.

1126) The zombie ant fungi can hijack an ant's central nervous and force the ant to do what it wants. When an ant contacts the fungal spores, the fungus infects the ant and quickly spreads throughout its body. Fungal cells in the ant's head release chemicals that hijack the ant's central nervous system. The fungus forces the ant to climb up vegetation and clamp down onto a leaf or twig before killing it. After the ant is dead, the fungus grows a spore releasing stalk out of the back of the ant's head to infect more ants on the ground below.

1127) One million people live under the streets of Beijing, China in bomb shelters built during the Cold War. When tensions eased, the government leased the bunkers to landlords who rented them to tenants who tend to be young people or migrant workers who can't afford other housing in the city.

1128) Poena cullei was an execution punishment in ancient Rome for killing your father; it consisted of being sewn up in a sack along with a monkey, a viper, a dog, and a cock and then being thrown into water. Before being put in the bag, the person was beaten with rods, and their head was covered in a bag made of wolf's hide.

1129) Born in 1773, Potoooooooo or later shortened to Pot8O's was one of the greatest racehorses ever and one of the three foundation sires of thoroughbreds today. His name was intended to be Potato or Potatoes, but the stable hand who wrote down his name didn't know how to spell potato and thought it was "pot" plus eight O's.

1130) Zugzwang is a situation in chess and other games where a player must move, but all moves are bad or put them at a disadvantage.

1131) Humans aren't either left brained or right brained as once thought; most behaviors and abilities require the right and left sides of the brain to work together. You have characteristics and abilities that define who you are, but they have nothing to do with which side of the brain you use more.

1132) Cheetahs can't roar; they can purr, meow, hiss, bark, and growl.

1133) Pareidolia is the term for seeing patterns in random data. Some common examples are seeing a likeness in the clouds or an image on the surface of the Moon.

1134) Robins can eat up to 14 feet of earthworms in a day.

1135) In 1898, Nikola Tesla created the first remote control that could control mechanical devices at a distance with radio waves. The first electronic television wasn't invented until 29 years later in 1927, and the first wireless television remote wasn't created until 1956.

1136) UY Scuti, a bright red supergiant star in the Scutum constellation about 9,500 light-years away, is believed to be the largest star in the Milky Way Galaxy and has a volume about 27.3 quadrillion times larger than the Earth. Its radius is about 1,700 times larger than the Sun.

1137) Adult humans have a diving reflex like other mammals and all air breathing vertebrates studied to date. The diving reflex is triggered when the nostrils become chilled and wet while holding your breath. The body reacts with slowed heart rate, redirection of blood to the vital organs to conserve oxygen, and a release of red blood cells stored in the spleen enabling the body to survive submersion for a longer time.

1138) The 55-foot diameter 10,000-ton meteor that struck Russia in 2013 had an estimated impact energy of 500 kilotons and affected an area of 77,000 square miles. The atomic bomb dropped on Hiroshima was about 33 times smaller at 15 kilotons of energy.

1139) Even rarer than a double rainbow, a twinned rainbow has two separate and concentric rainbow arcs splitting from a single base. Unlike a double rainbow, both rainbows have their colors in the same order. Twinned rainbows occur with a combination of different size raindrops; due to air resistance, raindrops flatten as they fall with larger drops flattening more. If there are two rain showers with different size drops, they can combine to form a twinned rainbow.

1140) Cicadas flex their muscles to buckle a series of ribs one after another to produce their loud sound. Every time a rib buckles, it produces a click; many clicks produce the buzzing sound. The series of ribs are called a tymbal.

1141) Lobsters do not have blood like vertebrate animals. The liquid found in their body which acts as blood is called hemolymph; it is colorless and turns blue when exposed to air due to oxygen reacting with the copper in the fluid.

1142) Submarines made their first war time appearance during the American Revolutionary War. *Turtle*, a submersible built by American David Bushnell in 1775, was used in an attempted attack on the British ship *Eagle* on Sept. 6, 1776. It was a one-man wooden craft which relied on a human-powered hand crank and foot treadle for propulsion. A pedal-operated water tank allowed it to submerge and surface, and lead ballast kept it upright in the water.

1143) *Law & Order: Special Victims Unit* is the only U.S. primetime drama ever to be spun off from two different shows. It spun off from *Law & Order* (1990), and the character of Detective John Munch came from *Homicide: Life on the Street* (1993).

1144) For humans, the rarest hair and eye color combination in the world is red hair with blue eyes which accounts for only about 0.17% of the population. The combination is so rare because both red hair and blue eyes are recessive traits where both parents must carry the gene for the child to have it.

1145) Astronomers have discovered the largest reservoir of water ever detected in the universe; it has the equivalent of 140 trillion times all the water in the Earth's oceans and surrounds a huge black hole more than 12 billion light-years away.

1146) In 1881, the U.S. had three presidents in one year. The year started with President Rutherford B. Hayes who was succeeded by James A. Garfield in March after his election, and then Chester A. Arthur, Garfield's vice president, became president in September after Garfield's assassination.

1147) Even though it is the third most common element in the Earth's crust, aluminum was more valuable than gold in the 1800s because it was so rare. Aluminum is almost never found in its pure form, and it is difficult to extract from ores, so prior to more efficient processes being developed to extract it, aluminum was quite rare. In the 1850s, aluminum was priced at $1,200 per kilogram, and gold was priced at $664 per kilogram.

1148) Colonel Tom Parker, Elvis Presley's manager, sold "I Hate Elvis" and other anti-Elvis buttons to also make money off people who didn't like his client.

1149) Sloths are good swimmers; using a version of a dog paddle, they can swim up to three times as fast as they move on land.

1150) In 1849, Elizabeth Blackwell was the first woman to earn a medical degree in America. She graduated first in her class at New York's Geneva College.

1151) Humans swallow on average twice a minute even while sleeping.

1152) The Amazon River has the largest discharge volume of any river in the world at an average of about 55 million gallons per second. Its discharge is larger than the next seven largest rivers in the world combined and accounts for 20% of the total global river discharge to the oceans.

1153) Victoria Island in the Canadian territory of Nunavut has the largest island in a lake on an island in a lake on an island in the world. Victoria Island is the eighth largest island in the world; the final island is four acres.

1154) Without the impact of gravity, astronauts can become up to two inches taller in space.

1155) Saying "God bless you" when someone sneezes can be traced to the 6th century and an order by Pope Gregory I. A pandemic was spreading across the eastern Roman Empire, and the first symptom was severe, chronic sneezing quickly followed by death. Pope Gregory urged people to pray for the sick and ordered that responses to sneezes should be "God bless you."

1156) The average major league baseball lasts for six pitches.

1157) The only performers to win consecutive acting Oscars are Luise Rainer (1936 and 1937), Spencer Tracy (1937 and 1938), Katharine Hepburn (1967 and 1968), Jason Robards (1976 and 1977), and Tom Hanks (1993 and 1994).

1158) In ancient Greece, prostitution was common and accepted and regulated. Prostitutes wore sandals that left the words "follow me" imprinted on the ground as they walked.

1159) Human infants can't produce tears when crying until they are one to three months old.

1160) More than 90% of your serotonin, the neurotransmitter that contributes to feelings of well-being and happiness, is produced in the digestive tract.

1161) A sneeze sounds different in different parts of the world. While Americans typically say "achoo!"; for Germans, it is "hatschi!", for

Spanish, it is "achis!", for Japanese, it is "hakashun!", for Russians, it is "apchkhi!", for French, it is "atchoum!"

1162) Jane Austen referenced baseball over 40 years before it was invented. In 1797 in her novel *Northanger Abbey*, Austen wrote, "It was not very wonderful that Catherine, who had nothing heroic about her, should prefer cricket, base-ball, riding on horseback, and running about the country at the age of fourteen, to books." Baseball was supposedly invented by Abner Doubleday in Cooperstown, New York, in 1839; however, there are other earlier references to baseball even in America. To avoid broken windows, a 1791 bylaw in Pittsfield, Massachusetts banned the playing of "wicket, cricket, baseball, batball, football, cat, fives or any other game or games with balls" within 80 yards of the town meeting house. The name was certainly in use many decades before the current game was invented; the question is how much different the game was.

1163) Overmorrow is the day after tomorrow.

1164) Human babies only blink once or twice per minute while adults blink about 10 times per minute on average.

1165) Forty-three buildings in New York City are so big that they have their own ZIP Code.

1166) Pigs are physically incapable of looking up towards the sky from a standing position.

1167) Whispering is harder on your vocal cords than normal speech.

1168) Floccinaucinihilipilification is one of the longer words in the English language and means the action of estimating something as worthless.

1169) The Tower of Pisa took 177 years to build, but it started leaning due to soil subsidence just 10 years after its completion in 1372. The lean was 5.5 degrees prior to a 2010 restoration which reduced it to 4 degrees.

1170) Prairie dogs greet each other by kissing; the kiss involves touching their teeth together to determine whether the prairie dog they are greeting is a member of their own social group.

1171) It took over 200,000 years for the world's human population to reach one billion, but it only took 200 more years to reach 7 billion.

1172) Lightning strikes the Earth's surface about 100 times per second.

1173) Cassowaries are the second largest bird in the world standing up to 6 feet tall and weighing up to 130 pounds. They are one of the most dangerous birds with a four-inch, dagger-like claw on each foot that can slice open a predator or threat with a single kick. They can also run up to 31 mph and jump 7 feet. They are native to the tropical forests of Papua New Guinea, Indonesia, and northeastern Australia.

1174) The Buddha you often see in statues is a Buddha and not the Buddha. The Buddha, Siddhartha Gautama, who founded Buddhism is not the same person as the typical fat Laughing Buddha who is based on an eccentric monk who lived around the 10th century. In Buddhism, the term Buddha is used for a person who has attained enlightenment through meditation.

1175) The reminiscence bump is the tendency to have increased recollection of events that occurred during adolescence and early adulthood. The bump occurs from about 16 to 25 years of age because memory storage is not consistent through time; it increases during times of change in self and life goals that typically happen during the reminiscence bump years.

1176) In 1771, future president James Madison was the first graduate student ever at Princeton University.

1177) Without an air circulation system, a flame in zero gravity, even in a pure oxygen environment, will extinguish itself. A typical flame produces light, heat, carbon dioxide and water vapor; the heat causes the combustion products to expand, lowering their density, and they rise allowing fresh, oxygen-containing air to get to the flame. In zero gravity, nether buoyancy or convection occur; therefore, the combustion products accumulate around the flame preventing oxygen from reaching it, and the flame goes out.

1178) Liechtenstein has a very low crime rate and only has a single prison with about 10 inmates; any criminal requiring a sentence of more than two years is sent to Austria.

1179) Lemurs in Madagascar capture large red millipedes to get a narcotic hit and ward off insects. When millipedes are picked up, they secrete a toxic combination of chemicals, including cyanide, as a defense mechanism. Lemurs pick up a millipede and bite it gently and throw it back on the ground; they rub the millipede secretion all over their fur which functions as a natural pesticide and wards off malaria carrying mosquitos. The secretion also acts as a narcotic which causes the lemurs to salivate profusely and enter a state of intoxication.

1180) The competition between dogs and cats goes back millions of years; about 20 million years ago in North America, it appears that early cats led to the extinction of most of the ancient dogs.

1181) Astronauts in space are exposed to radiation that is the equivalent of up to 6,000 chest x-rays.

1182) The largest single living organism in the world is a honey mushroom in Malheur National Forest in Oregon that covers more than three square miles, weighs at least 7,500 tons, and is at least 2,000 years old. For most of the year, the honey mushroom is a thin white layer of fungus that spreads up under a tree's bark and rots its roots eventually killing the tree over possibly decades. DNA testing has confirmed it is the same organism that has spread from a single location thousands of years ago.

1183) In seven years as a lifeguard at Lowell Park in Dixon, Illinois, future president Ronald Reagan was credited with saving 77 people from drowning in the waters of the Rock River. He started his lifeguard position at the age of 15.

1184) The Wright brothers only flew together once in 1910; otherwise, their father made them promise they would never fly together in case an accident would take them both.

1185) Thomas Andrews, one of the designers of the *Titanic*, was on board when it went down, and his body was never recovered. His design suggestions that the ship have 46 lifeboats instead of the 20 it had, a double hull, and a larger number of watertight bulkheads were overruled.

1186) The oldest known advertising dates from about 3,000 BC in Thebes, Greece where a fabric seller announced a reward for the return of his slave to his store where the most beautiful fabrics are woven for each person's taste.

1187) In 1977, the USSR started a televised song contest that allowed viewers to vote by turning on their light switches. The show was called *Intervision* and was like *Eurovision* but designed for the Eastern Bloc countries. Since phones were rare in the USSR at the time, people voted by turning their light switches on for their favorites. Mail was too slow, and people didn't trust paper ballots anyway, so they arranged with the state power authorities to measure the power spikes and report them to determine points for each contestant.

1188) More than 80% of marriages in history might have been between second or closer cousins. Ancient times had fewer people dispersed over wide areas, so inbreeding was inevitable.

1189) Genghis Khan once ordered his own army to eat every tenth man. In 1214, Khan laid siege to the city of Chungdu, capital of the Chinese Jin empire. The siege went on for a long time, and supplies were short for the Mongols; they were also ravaged by plague. Khan ordered that every tenth man be sacrificed to feed the others. Khan later personally abandoned the siege leaving it to one of his generals, and Chungdu eventually fell in 1215.

1190) The longest gloved boxing match in history was in 1893 and lasted for 110 three-minute rounds for a total of 7 hours and 19 minutes. It was a lightweight match between Andy Bowen and Jack Burke in New Orleans, Louisiana and began around 9 pm and finished after 4 am. There was no winner as both fighters were too exhausted to continue.

1191) The swastika has been around for over 3,000 years and commonly symbolized goodness and luck until its use by the Nazis in Germany. It has been used by cultures all over the world including early Christians, Jews, Hindus, and Buddhists.

1192) It wasn't always pink for girls and blue for boys; it was even reversed at one time. Pink for girls and blue for boys didn't really take hold until the middle of the 20th century. Earlier, it was common practice for children to wear gender neutral mostly white clothing. When department stores started marketing gender specific colors, some early advertising suggested pink for boys since it was considered a stronger color and blue for girls since it was more delicate and daintier.

1193) The name Lego is an abbreviation of the Danish words "leg godt" meaning "play well."

1194) Tiny mammals lived alongside dinosaurs for more than 150 million years. They were small nocturnal animals, and they remained relatively small until the demise of the dinosaurs 65 million years ago left more niches for them to fill.

1195) Although it had been proposed in some form for over 50 years, the scientific community didn't agree on plate tectonics until 1967, two years before we landed on the Moon.

1196) Established in 1636, Harvard didn't offer calculus classes for the first few years because it hadn't been invented yet.

1197) The drug ecstasy was invented by Merck in 1912. Merck wanted to develop something to stop abnormal bleeding, and it synthesized MDMA to avoid a Bayer patent. There was no real interest in it at the time, and it wasn't until 1975 that he psychoactive effects of the drug were seriously considered.

1198) The Brooklyn Bridge was under construction the year of Custer's defeat at the Battle of Little Bighorn in 1876.

1199) On average, people burn about 0.42 calories an hour per pound of body weight while sleeping, so a 150-pound person burns about 63 calories per hour sleeping.

1200) Martin Van Buren is the only U.S. president that did not speak English as their first language. Van Buren, who was president from 1837-1841, grew up in the Dutch community of Kinderhook, New York and spoke Dutch as a child; he learned English as a second language while attending school.

Made in the USA
Middletown, DE
14 May 2020